Virtue of Disobedience

Also by Jake Highton

Virtue of Disobedience

Jake Highton

Emeritus journalism professor
from the University of Nevada, Reno.

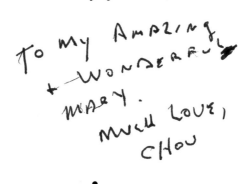

world vision
p u b l i s h i n g

Reno, Nevada

Sketch of Jake Highton
by Jennifer Klein of the Sparks Tribune.

Cover Photo: Oscar Wilde

World Vision Publishing
© 2016 by World Vision Publishing. All rights reserved
Printed in United States of America
10 09 08 07 06   16 15 14 13 12 11 10

Library of Congress Catalog Card Number: 2016949301

Highton, Jake
A Collection of Newspaper Columns

ISBN 978-0-9961365-2-5

Epigraph

Disobedience, in the eyes of anyone who has read history, is man's original virtue. It is through disobedience that progress has been made, through disobedience and through rebellion.

The Soul of Man Under Socialism
Oscar Wilde

Author's Notes

Most of these columns appeared in the weekly Sparks Tribune and the Reno News & Review. Thanks to both papers for courageously publishing columns and articles that no other newspaper or magazine would have printed.

———

Oscar Wilde, one of my all-time favorite people in history. Brilliant, witty, wise. Epigramist. Versatile: playwright, short-story writer, novelist, poet, social critic, essayist and book reviewer. Marvelous conversationalist. Classicist. Scholar. Dandy. Esthete. Humanist.

Oscar Wilde, one of the greatest multi-faced geniuses ever to grace the Earth.

On entering America in 1882 for a tour he purportedly told a custom official: "I have nothing to declare except my genius." Whether fact or fiction, it is so typical of what Wilde might have quipped.

He was right about Shakespeare, "the most purely human of all the great artists."

He wrote truly: "Out of the carpenter's shop at Nazareth had come a personality infinitely greater than any made of myth or legend. 'He that is without sin among you let him first cast a stone at her,' Jesus said. It is worthwhile living to have said only that."

He relates prison sorrow in his "The Ballad of Reading Gaol": "And alien tears will fill for him / Pity's long broken urn. / For his mourners will be outcast men.

Contents

Politics and Policies

Nation needs whistleblowers

Now we have President Obama warring on whistleblowers, bringing ridiculous charges in nine cases involving alleged misuse of classified information.

John Hanrahan, in an analytical article for Truthout, declares that both parties "have either kept silent or cheered on the Obama administration's unprecedented crackdown on whistleblowers. On the question of keeping Americans in the dark and of punishing whistleblowers who dare to enlighten them, we have bipartisan authoritarianism."

Madame Clinton suggests: "Edward Snowden and other national-security whistleblowers should go through channels to express concerns about military surveillance issues." Nonsense.

She adds: "Snowden's disclosures damaged national security by providing information to terrorist networks." More nonsense.

Manning persecution

Meanwhile, the Pentagon is persecuting whistleblower Chelsea Manning. The Army is threatening her with indefinite solitary confinement for such absurd "crimes" as having "expired" toothpaste and possessing a copy of Vanity Fair featuring Caitlyn Jenner. (The former Bruce Jenner won the men's decathlon for America at the 1976 Olympics.)

A three-member military board last month sentenced Manning to 21 days of "recreational" restriction: no gym, no library and no stepping outdoors. She was denied counsel during a four-hour, closed-door hearing. She was sentenced to 35 years in military prison in Fort Leavenworth in Kansas for espionage. She endured solitary confinement in Kuwait and Quantico, Virginia.

Manning's real "crime": leaking more than 700

documents revealing that the Pentagon failed to investigate torture, rape and abuse by the military in Iraq.

She was diagnosed with gender dysphoria in 2010. Behind bars she has become an outspoken opponent of the crimes of the U.S. military and advocate of transgender rights.

Papal plaudits undeserved

Pope Francis, papal rock star, has won worldwide praise for being a nice guy. But that is hardly praiseworthy. The sad truth is that the pope has changed none of the musty doctrines of the Roman Catholic Church.

Francis made a temporary absolution offering to Catholics "who bear in their heart the scar" of abortion and repent during the upcoming Jubilee or Holy Year.

Katie Klabusich in a Truthout news analysis countered that 95 percent of Catholics have neither struggled over nor regretted their abortions. It is not the "existential or moral ordeal" characterized by the pope.

"I grew up Catholic and attended a Jesuit university," Erin Matson, co-director of the reproductive justice organization, ReproAction, said.

"The official teachings of the Catholic Church on sexuality, including but not limited to abortion, harm people around the world," he pointed out. "The views of the Vatican are deeply out of step with the views of Catholics.

"Women who have had abortions have done nothing wrong. They have nothing to apologize for. We can't lose sight of the fact that Pope Francis is not changing any doctrine on abortion."

The Rev. Harry Knox, president of the Religious Coalition for Reproductive Choice, is blunt: Francis starts off with compassion "but quickly turns to more shame for women."

"Women have abortions for many reasons," he noted. "What a woman really needs from her clergy is someone ready and able to have deep pastoral conversations about the decision."

One in three Catholic women have had one or more abortions. U.S. Catholic women oppose criminalizing abortion by a margin of 2-1. This is the reality of Catholic women's lives, not some moldy papal decree.

More reactionaryism: the church is adamantly against birth control yet most Catholics use it. Garry Wills, Catholic writer, ridicules the idea that using a contraceptive is "a mortal sin for which Catholics would go to hell if they died unrepentant."

Still more reactionaryism: the church is woefully short of priests but will not allow women into the priesthood. It deems women unequal to men. Sister Louise Akers, head of the Sisters of Charity, rightly calls the Catholic Church "the last bastion of sexism."

And yet more backwardness: the church insists that priests be celibate. Celibacy is unnatural. Most priestly pedophilia can be attributed to celibacy. The church doesn't allow divorced Catholics to take communion. It should. Communion is central to Catholicism.

And still more backward doctrines: the church prohibits the use of condoms even to prevent AIDS--a clear example of head-in-the-sand dogma. The church opposes premarital sex, a view contrary to human nature and therefore practiced by most Catholics.

And still more dithering: the streamlined annulment procedure recently unveiled by the pope supposedly simplifies the arduous gauntlet of red tape. A worthwhile outcome is dubious.

Annulment proceedings can take a year or more and cost upwards of $1,000 in "bribes" to annulling bishops. Francis asks that annulments be granted free. Asking is not promulgating.

The church needs genuine reform, not cosmetics.

Pope Francis recently canonized Junipero Serra, founder of Spanish missions in California. He called him "a friend of humanity." Keener judgment would call Serra unworthy of sainthood.

His missionaries tried to convert Indians to Christianity. Serra required Indians to learn Spanish. He advocated using whips to lash those who spoke the native language and followed native culture. Indians were forced to labor under brutal and sometimes fatal conditions.

Sainthood should not be bestowed on someone who forces conversion at the end of a whip.

Sparks Tribune, Sept. 22, 2015

U.S. backs rights violations

The American public is aware of the endless wars perpetuated by the United States. But it seems unaware of the nation's support for countries with gross human rights violations.

Namely: Egypt, which specializes in murder, torture, "enforced disappearances" and suppression of all dissent.

The Egyptian government under President Fattah al-Sisi has shut down the nation's human rights organization and imposed a reign of terror.

It abducts a disabled woman photographer for two weeks as one of thousands of brutalities carried out by military, police and state security forces. An Italian PhD student, found half-naked by a roadside, was slowly killed by torture carried out by state security forces.

Jessica Winegar, in a Truthout op-ed interpretive article, reports: "From 1948 to 2015 the U.S. gave $76 billion in aid to Egypt, the vast majority earmarked for the military. Since 1987 this has equaled $1.3 billion a year."

In short, a far cry from the millions of Egyptians celebrating in Tahrir Square the overthrow of a tyrant in 2011 with the exultant cry: "bread, freedom and social justice." The U.S. backed the dictator, arguing falsely that the massive aid was necessary to ensure regional security.

Winegar concludes: "The U.S. is mainly responsible for creating and sustaining the vast military machine that puts a stranglehold on the Egyptian people."

Afghanistan Opium War

The U.S. fought for 15 years in Afghanistan, the longest war in its history. It deployed 100,000 soldiers. About 2,200 of them were killed. It spent more than a trillion dollars in military operations, expended a hundred billion more on nation-building and reconstruction. And,

7

it helped raise, fund, equip and train an army of 350,000 Afghans.

Yet Alfred McCoy in a news analysis on TomDispatch says the U.S. stands on the brink of defeat in Afghanistan. Why?

"Washington's massive military juggernaut has been stopped dead in its steel tracks by a pink flower, the opium poppy," McCoy writes. "For more than three decades in Afghanistan, Washington's military operations have succeeded only when they fit into Central Asia's illicit traffic in opium.

"The first U.S. intervention there succeeded because the surrogate war the CIA launched in 1979 to expel the Soviets coincided with Afghan allies using the swelling drug trade to sustain the fight.

"American military technology transformed this remote, landlocked nation into the world's first narco-state, a country where illicit drugs dominate the economy, define political choices and determine the fate of military interventions."

Another Humanitarian Disaster

President Obama needed to placate Saudi Arabia after he made a deal with Iran, the Saudi's archenemy. So Obama gave his approval for the Pentagon to support a Saudi military campaign.

"But a year later the war has been a humanitarian disaster for Yemen," the New York Times reported. "And it also shows the perils of Obama's push to get Middle Eastern countries to take on bigger military roles in the neighborhood."

Sen. Christopher Murphy, a Connecticut Democrat on the Foreign Relations Committee, is blunt: "As I read about the conflict in Yemen, I have a hard time figuring out what the U.S. national security interests are."

So do millions of Americans.

Bogus electric highway

The 450-miles of Highway 95 between Reno and Las Vegas will not be the magnificent "electric highway" that Nevada's Governor Sandoval boasts of. The governor's notion was thoroughly demolished recently by Sparks Tribune columnist, Thomas Mitchell.

Sandoval dedicated the first electric car recharging station in Beatty. Three more are planned. But, but, but. Let Mitchell tell the truth of the bogus electric highway:

"Electric cars have a range of 100 miles before recharging. The distance from downtown Las Vegas to Beatty is 120 miles. Then if you reach the recharging station it might require as much as four hours to recharge.

"If you reach Goldfield you need a tow truck to take you 26 miles to get to the next recharging station--if and when it is built in Tonopah.

"After a layover in Tonopah, someday, you might get as far as Mina or Luning before calling for a tow truck to the next planned station in Hawthorne--103 miles from Tonopah."

You get the idea. Same problem in Fallon--if and when the Fallon recharging station ever gets built.

Sandoval, bragging it is the first electric highway in the United States, plans a phase two with recharging stations in Fernley, Lovelock, Winnemucca, Battle Mountain and Elko.

His dream is a nightmare.

Columnist Mitchell's footnote: "Tesla Motors, the recipient of $1.3 billion in state tax abatements and credits for its battery factory in Sparks, does have models that are supposed to get 200 miles per charge--costing $75,000."

Sparks Tribune, March 22, 2016

Revenge behind Assange 'captivity'

The Julian Assange detention has nothing to do with sexual misconduct and everything to do with the Pentagon desire to exact revenge for his WikiLeaks exposure of U.S. crimes in Iraq and Afghanistan.

Namely, wholesale killings of civilians and contempt for sovereignty and international law.

Whistleblowing is not unconstitutional. As a presidential candidate in 2008, constitutional law professor Barack Obama lauded whistleblowers as "part of a healthy democracy" and declared they "must be protected from reprisal."

John Pilger, in a Truthout Op-Ed analysis of the Assange case, recently called it one of the epic injustices of our time. Assange has been living in the Ecuadorean embassy London for five years but now the case against him appears to be unraveling.

The United Nations group that decides compliance with international human rights obligations has ruled that Assange has been detained unlawfully by Sweden and Britain. The British parliament has discredited his "captivity." The chief prosecutor in Stockholm, Eva Finne, dismissed the case against Assange.

"There is no reason to suspect he has committed rape," Finne said. Moreover, one of the woman involved in the case said the police fabricated evidence, railroaded her and protested that she "did not want to accuse Assange of anything."

But the Pentagon is adamant about whistleblowers. One whistleblower, Chelsea Manning, was sentenced to 35 years in prison and tortured during her pre-trial detention. (Thirty-five years for whistleblowing!)

Another leaker, Edward Snowden, released documents revealing that Assange is on a U.S. "manhunt target list." Vice President Biden calls Assange a "cyber terrorist."

In Alexandria, Va., a secret grand jury attempted to concoct a crime against Assange even though he is an Australian citizen. And, through it all, the United States insists the Assange case is a state secret.

John Pilger, in his analysis, hails "tiny, brave Ecuador" for granting asylum to Assange when the gutless politicians of Australia, in collusion with America, would not.

Pilger concludes with a stinging indictment of the United States:

"The decent world owes much to Julian Assange. He told us how indecent power behaves in secret, how it lies and manipulates and engages in great acts of violence, sustaining wars that kill and maim and turn millions into refugees.

"Telling us the truth alone should earn Assange his freedom. Justice is his right."

Court's Pols Block Global Warming

The Supreme Court recent decision to put a hold on President Obama's global warming plan is what a New York Times editorial calls extraordinary.

It may be that but it is business as usual for a majority of the court blocking any progress.

The Obama administration wants to combat global warming by curbing carbon emissions from coal-fired plants. Its Clean Power Plan requires states to make major cuts in greenhouse gas emissions from their electricity producers. The target for reduced emissions is 25 percent.

A majority of Americans, including many Republicans, agree that global warming is, or will be, a serious threat.

Chief Justice Roberts claims that the court is viewed unfairly as just another political branch. It is not unfair. He insists that the court doesn't work as "Democrats or Republicans." But it does.

The GOP commands the court. It's just that Roberts never admits the biases of his commanding politicians.

A brief court order, by a 5-4 vote, temporarily blocked the global-warming plan. The liberal bloc of four dissented from an unprecedented Supreme Court order.

Scotus had never before granted a request to halt a regulation before its legal fate had been decided by lower federal district and appeals courts. (The Environmental Protection Agency issued the order last summer for states to make major cuts in greenhouse gas pollution.)

Jody Freeman, a Harvard law professor and former environmental counsel for the Obama administration, called the ruling "a stunning development."

Freeman cited her two chief concerns: "a high degree of initial judicial skepticism" and raising "serious questions from nations that signed the landmark climate-change."

Twenty-nine states and dozens of corporations and industry groups filed suit, labeling it a federal power grab by the EPA.

But Solicitor General Donald Verrilli called "climate change the most significant environmental challenge of our day, one that is already affecting national public health, welfare and the environment."

He's absolutely right. But far too many Americans think climate change is an idea or story expounded by many people but not true. A myth.

Sparks Tribune, Feb. 23, 2016

Obama's brilliant deal

The United States is Iran's Great Satan
Ayatollahs of Iran

It's hardly surprising that Iranians with long memories and good history classes have deep-seated hatred of America. The United States, with the help of Britain, engineered a coup in 1953 that overthrew the democratically elected Iranian prime minister, Mohammad Mossaddegh.

Why? He was a leftist who nationalized the oil industry and called for independence from all foreign powers. His target: the Anglo-Iranian Oil Co. The United States simply could not tolerate that. The CIA and British intelligence orchestrated his ouster and re-installed the Shah, a dictator hated by most Iranians.

Yet today we find the head of Iran, Supreme Leader Ayatollah Khamenei, making a pact with the supreme leader of Satan, President Obama.

It was a brilliant deal, limiting Iran's nuclear ability for at least 10 years in return for lifting Iranian oil and financial sanctions. It could be one of the most important diplomatic accords in diplomatic history.

As the New York Times put it an editorial, "it has the ability to reshape Middle East politics."

But the prime minister of Israel, Bibi Netanyahu, does not think so. He denounced the proposal "as a historic mistake and a dangerous compromise, paving the way for an arsenal of multiple bombs."

He called Iran a rogue regime, a terrorist regime, "one that threatens the very existence of Israel. Lifting sanctions would reward it with hundreds of billions of dollars, cash bonuses to fuel Iran's worldwide terrorism."

Oh, my, the apocalypse now! Netanyahu did not say Israel already has an atomic bomb in its extensive nuclear arsenal. He did not mention that Israel is a rogue nation.

Another overreacting foe: the U.S. Congress. Congressional critics, horrified by the accord, are urging Congress to vote against it.

But Obama has the upper hand: veto of any congressional law he opposes. Overriding a veto requires a two-thirds vote, which is practically impossible because of the many Democrats backing the pact.

Still other overreactors: the 50 Republican candidates for the presidency, most of them vying to see who can revile it most.

Congress has 90 days to review the deal, the Iranian parliament 80. The United Nations Security Council has already approved the accord, 15-0. The resolution backs the lifting of sanctions against Iran. Still another approver of the deal: the European Union.

Here are some of the elements of the accord as listed by the New York Times:
• Iran will be allowed to produce a small amount of uranium enriched at low levels but not suitable for an atomic bomb.
• If Tehran abides by the agreement if will not have enough material or the centrifuge to make an atomic bomb.
• The deal requires Iran to reduce its stockpile of low-enriched uranium by 98 percent.
• Inspectors can ask to visit sites where they suspect nuclear activity.
• The accord contains provisions for "snapback" sanctions if a panel of nations should detect Iranian cheating. (The panelists: Russia, China, Britain, France and Germany.)
• But Iran, more than twice the size of Texas, poses challenges for nuclear inspection with so many underground sites.
• Yet Iran has agreed to transform its deeply buried plant at Fordo into a center for science research. Another uranium plant, Natanz, is to be cut back but not shut down.
• Yes, Iran can cheat but Obama has "the faith" and so we

should too. Besides, the pact is designed so Iran cannot get away with cheating.

This columnist has constantly criticized President Obama but this accord deserves the highest praise.

Fraud exposed

A hidden-camera video recently released purported to show that Planned Parenthood (PP) illegally sells tissues from aborted fetuses. It's a fraud, one of a series of unrelenting attacks on PP whose clinics serve millions of people.

Right-wing politicians, howling to defund PP, issued a nine-minute version of a two-hour interview with PP executives. The truth was edited out.

The New York Times editorialized: "Anti-abortion groups have long sought to defund PP even though no federal money is used to provide abortions. But that hasn't stopped their efforts to shut down the clinics, which provide services like contraception and cancer screening."

Cecile Richards, president of the Planned Parenthood Federation of America, said recently that its donation program follows all laws and ethical guidelines.

"PP stands behind its work to help women and their families donate tissue for medical research," she declared. "The Center for Medical Progress video campaign is a dishonest attempt to make legal, voluntary and potentially life-saving donations appear nefarious and illegal."

PP advocates the right to clean, safe abortions. Sen. Rand Paul of Kentucky calls that abhorrent. But it is Paul who is abhorrent.

Sparks Tribune, Aug. 4, 2015

Filibuster tarnishes Reid

Sen. Harry Reid, after 50 years in Nevada politics, will leave office with one terrible stain: keeping in place the dreadful filibuster.

Yes, he did succeed in getting 60 votes to thwart a filibuster against Obamacare. Yes, he did keep nuclear waste storage out of Nevada. Yes, he did fight the pollution of the coal-energy barons. And yes, when he was still in the House, he fought for the Great Basin National Park in Nevada. Jon Ralston of Politico magazine called the park "a true wilderness jewel which would not exist if it hadn't been for him."

Fine achievements. Yet Reid, who will not seek a fifth term next year, refused to end the filibuster.

The Senate tactic, proposed by Vice President Aaron Burr, was adopted in 1806. It was modified several times since but to this day is basically unchanged: a supermajority of 60 senators rules, not the majority of 51 that should decide legislation in a purported democracy.

Reid--and Reid alone--is responsible for today's filibuster obstructionism.

Reid never studied the history of the filibuster. The Senate historian told him he had sole authority to end the filibuster. Reid ignored him. One of Reid's aides called a Nevada specialist on the history of the filibuster. He was told Reid had sole authority to act. Reid and the aide ignored the wisdom of the expert.

Reid was majority leader 12 years when the Democrats controlled the Senate. At the first session of a new Congress all he had to do was ask for a simple majority vote to approve legislation. He did not, tarnishing his reputation and damaging the nation.

Republicans used the filibuster more than 360 times while Reid was majority leader. Some of the "vetoes" were progressive measures like women's pay equality. The bill passed, 52-47, but could not muster 60 votes to break a filibuster.

Reactionary Republicans defeated the Fairness Pay bill at a time when women were earning 77 cents to every $1 earned by men in comparable jobs and of comparable experience.

As a politician Reid was lucky. Only one of his Senate opponents was strong. The weakest was Sharron Angle in 2010. She was an absurd right-winger and Christian fundamentalist. John Ensign was the strongest. In 1998 he lost by just 428 votes out of 436,000 cast.

Reid was a dull pol. But he flashed a dry wit in announcing his retirement. A reporter asked him if he would retire to Searchlight, a desert crossroad in southern Nevada where Reid was born 75 years ago.

He answered the question emphatically with a question: "Have you ever been to Searchlight?"

Electoral College fraud

Speaking of undemocratic and unconstitutional matters in this "exceptional" nation, the United States clings to the antiquated Electoral College (EC).

Just two states, Maine and Nebraska, do not award all their electoral votes to the statewide election winner. That is less than a drop in the bucket. The EC outrage has 48 states give all their electoral votes to the presidential candidate that wins the state--even if only by 10 votes.

No other country in the world elects its president in this bizarre and unfair way.

Moreover, the Constitution is also flawed in giving six small-population states two U.S. senators even though they have fewer than a million people. Namely: Wyoming, Vermont, North Dakota, Alaska, South Dakota and Delaware. Eight states have two senators with fewer than two million people. Namely: Montana, Rhode Island,

New Hampshire, Maine, Hawaii, Idaho, West Virginia and Nebraska.

The EC also can give victory to the presidential candidate who wins far fewer popular votes. Al Gore garnered 550,000 more votes than G.W. Bush in 2000. In a democratic country he would have won the presidency.

Florida election officials blundered much of the statewide tally so the Florida Supreme Court ordered a machine recount as mandated by state law. But the U.S. Supreme Court stepped in, doing what it was not asked. It stole the election for Bush. Four justices dissented from a highly partisan 5-4 vote. One of the dissenters, John Paul Stevens, wrote:

"The majority position is wholly without merit. The endorsement of that position can only lend credence to the most cynical appraisal of judges throughout the land. The loser here is the nation's confidence in the justices as impartial guardians of the rule of law."

The Supreme Court had pulled off the greatest theft in U.S. political history.

Sparks Tribune, April 14, 2015

Elect Bernie Sanders president
for good of nation

Among the welter of Republican candidates and the few Democrats running for president, Bernie Sanders is far and away the best.

Senator Sanders, Vermont Democrat, socialist and presidential candidate, recently declared that immigrants should be welcomed and assimilated, not stigmatized and criminalized, as some Republicans insist on.

Sanders would protect young immigrants and their parents from deportation. He would designate them as permanent legal residents--humane treatment for 11 million unauthorized immigrants.

His election platform calls for another political revolution, the most progressive since Franklin Roosevelt in the 1930s and 1940s.

More items in Sander's forward-looking agenda:

• Wages: "Millions of Americans are working for starvation wages. The federal minimum wage is $7.25 an hour. It should be $15 an hour."

• Taxes: "The skyrocketing of income and wealth inequality is grotesque and immoral. It serves the One Percent and harms the 99 percent. Congress votes for the rich at the expense of the vast majority."

• Universal health: "America is the only major country without universal national health care, a gross embarrassment for the wealthiest nation in the world."

• Wall Street: "Its six major financial institutions have assets worth 60 percent of our Gross National Product, issue 35 percent of mortgages and two-thirds of credit cards. This excess is spurred by a tax system rigged for the rich. The big corporations earn billions in profits, stash the money in tax havens abroad and pay nothing in federal income taxes. Billionaire hedge fund managers pay a lower tax rate than teachers or nurses."

• Campaign finance: "As a result of the Supreme Court ruling in Citizens United (2010), billionaires spend an exorbitant amount for candidates and elections. This undermines democracy."

• Climate control "If we do not act boldly on climate change, the planet we leave our grandchildren may be uninhabitable. The scientific community is nearly unanimous that climate change, caused by human beings, is already damaging the planet."

• Infrastructure: "Congress refuses to appropriate the necessary funds to rebuild our crumbling roads, bridges, railroads, airports, water systems, wastewater plants, dams and levies."

The New York Times in October declared Hillary Clinton "the unrivaled leader in the Democratic contest." Meanwhile, most of the mainstream newspapers declared that Sanders was far too radical for most American voters."

Unrivaled? Too radical? FAIR, media watchdog, noted in its December newsletter, Extra, that in the first primary state, New Hampshire, Clinton *trailed* Sanders by two points in one poll. Pollsters can be wrong and November is many months away. But it is clear that Sanders is very much in the race.

So vote fearlessly for Sanders!

Rose Belongs in Hall of Fame

Pete Rose is banned from baseball for the terrible wrong of gambling on games as a player and manager. But he should not be barred from the Hall of Fame.

Rose's record fairly screams for admission to the Hall. As a player for the Cincinnati Reds he got 4,256 hits, more than any player in history. He won three batting titles, was selected for the All-Star game 17 times and played in three World Series.

His uniform, No. 14, is already in the Hall of Fame at Cooperstown, N.Y. So is a video of his hit No. 4,192, which broke the record of the great Ty Cobb, another rough-and-tumble player like Rose.

It's the Hall of Fame, for god's sake, not the hall of shame.

Believe it or Not

A ridiculous law in Thailand makes it a crime to insult the monarchy, including his majesty's dog.

In a case brought before a Thai military court in Bangkok, workman Thanakorn Siripaiboon was charged with making a sarcastic remark on the Internet about the king's pet. He also faces charges of sedition, if you can believe it. Moreover, the so-called insult was not disclosed, presumably in the interest of national security.

But lèse majesté, a crime against a sovereign, is not a laughing matter in Thailand. According to the New York Times, the worker faces 37 years in prison.

In 2015 a prominent scholar in Thailand was accused of insulting a king who died four centuries earlier. Even an American ambassador to Thailand was investigated for "impiety" several years ago.

By Thailand standards, the archaic British royals are not that absurd.

Sparks Tribune, Jan. 5, 2016

Humanity's basic rule is war

Don't believe a word President Obama says. He promises one thing today then changes his mind later.

He promised repeatedly to have no "boots on the ground" in Syria. Now he's reversing course. Oh, Obama says, it's only 50 Special Operations forces. But we've heard that story before. Start small then gradually expand involvement.

Even without the broken promise, Americans have to wonder why U.S. troops are in Syria just as they wondered why the U.S. launched a bombing campaign on the Islamic State (ISIS) in Syria in 2014.

It's all war, war, war with Obama even though the U.S. has no business fighting in the Middle East.

As United Nations Secretary-General Ban Ki-moon declared recently: "The fighting must stop in Syria. There is no military solution to constant wars whether from Afghanistan to Central Africa, from Ukraine to Yemen. Combatants and those who control them are defying humanity's most basic rules."

Ki-moon is right about stopping wars but his plea for humanity is wrong. Humanity's basic rule is war.

Since last year 10 nations have dropped bombs in Syria: the United States, Russia, Britain, Canada, France, Australia, Turkey, Israel, the United Arab Emirates and Jordan.

Obama has escalated the U.S. "duty to make war," recently sending 12 F-15s to the Incirlik Air Base in Turkey and intensifying the air war in Syria. The Pentagon acted on Syria with the excuse that a U.S. commando was killed in Iraq.

This was the president who warned in 2014 that the U.S. must "always guard against mission creep." Yet he keeps creeping: fighting in Iraq, Syria, Afghanistan and drone striking from Pakistan to Yemen.

The U.S. has 3,600 U.S. troops in an Iraq America once quit. Obama is becoming the most infamous mission creeper in history.

Nick Turse, an expert on the military, notes that U.S. elite forces are "deployed in a record-shattering 147 countries." It is involved in more than 90 percent of Africa's 54 nations, he notes, adding: "The U.S. command carried out 674 missions across the African continent last year, an average of nearly two a day."

Tom Engelhardt in a TomDispatch op-ed estimates that $50 billion in taxpayer money has been lost to fraud and waste in Iraq and Afghanistan under the American reconstruction program.

"In Iraq a $75 million police academy, initially hailed as crucial to U.S. efforts to prepare Iraqis to take control of the country's security, flopped," Engelhardt writes. "It was so poorly constructed that it proved a health hazard. Feces and urine rained from ceilings of the student barracks.

"Roads were built to nowhere. A chicken-processing plant built in Iraq for $2.58 million never plucked a chicken and sent it to market." America sent millions of dollars worth of aid to Afghanistan never accounted for: 465,000 in small arms, rifles, machine guns and grenade launchers.

The tales of fraud and waste told by Engelhardt are seemingly endless. But it is revenge for the unjust U.S. invasions of Iraq and Afghanistan.

In Cuba, Obama is not making war but he is not making peace either. The United Nations General Assembly recently passed a resolution condemning the continued U.S. commercial, economic and financial Cuban embargo.

The vote was 191-2. The United States voted no. It was joined by Israel, which is protected by the U.S. and hence always its voting toady.

The U.S. Deputy Ambassador to the U.N., Ronald Godard, said the resolution "falls short of the spirit of engagement that President Obama has championed." What a champion!

Every year since 1992 the U.S. has voted no on those resolutions, ignoring as usual international consensus. Since Russia is bombing in Syria against Syrian President Bashar al-Assad, Obama figures the U.S. should drop bombs too, keeping the Cold War alive.

The European Parliaments in Brussels passed a resolution urging the 28 nations of the European Union to recognize Edward Snowden as a "whistle-blower and international human rights defender" who should not be prosecuted.

Snowden, who is living in Russia on a three-year residency permit, has sharply criticized the United States for eavesdropping and wiretapping. Obama will have none of it. Snowden's exposure of U.S. crimes is beyond the pale to him.

And here's another broken promise. Obama vowed to close Guantánamo Bay prison in Cuba if he was elected in 2008. It's still open, costing $2.5 million a year per detainee.

Again in January 2009 Obama vowed to issue an executive order shutting down Gitmo in one year. He had the constitutional authority to do so. He did not. Then after Congress passed a bill forbidding transfer of prisoners to the U.S., he threatened to veto the measure. But the gutless Obama caved in, signing the bill.

Gitmo is no threat to national security. Prisoners are held without charges and trials, violating sacred American principles. Above all, as Sen. Dianne Feinstein of California and vice-chair of the Select Committee on Intelligence declared: "it's a huge waste of money."

Yet the House in Congress recently approved a defense bill barring Obama from closing Gitmo. The action leaves Senate Democrats and a few sane Senate Republicans as the last hope for closing the prison.

Obama 'Vetoes' Pipeline

Give the warmonger his due: praise for his emphatic no to Keystone XL, proposed oil pipeline from Alberta, Canada. Obama linked the pipeline "veto" with global warming.

The pipeline when completed would have carried 800,000 barrels of oil a day from the tar sands in Alberta, Canada, to refineries on the Gulf Coast. The pipeline would have caused frightful pollution, pouring dangerous levels of carbon dioxide into the atmosphere.

"America is now a global leader when it comes to taking serious action to fight climate change," Obama rightly declared.

Sparks Tribune, Nov, 17, 2015

Puritanical NFL upholds
ban on medical marijuana

Twenty-three states and the District of Columbia have legalized medical marijuana. Four states and D.C. have legalized pot for recreational uses. But the puritanical National Football League refuses to lift the ban on marijuana.

Eugene Monroe, in a seven-year NFL career as an offensive forward, has had concussions, several shoulder injuries, ankle sprains and the terrible pounding of line play.

He uses medical cannabis to ease that chronic pain but NFL Commissioner Roger Goodell says no based on his own blind medical advisers. Monroe rightly castigates Goodell for that blindness. Here's how serious Monroe is: he has contributed $10,000 for research on medical marijuana and urged other players to do likewise.

Meanwhile we have the absurd Alabama law of sentencing a 75-year-old disabled veteran to prison for life for growing three dozen marijuana plants. He, too, is using cannabis to ease chronic pain, not to sell it.

But since the vet, Lee Brooker, was convicted of a felony in Florida 20 years earlier, Alabama law required a life sentence. This is a violation of the Eighth Amendment barring cruel and unusual punishment.

Ray Moore, chief justice of the Alabama Supreme Court, called Brooker's sentence "excessive and unjustified," revealing "grave flaws" in Alabama's sentencing law.

It sure does. But it is typical of repressive Southern laws on abortion, voting rights, gays and transgenders.

Voting Rights Lose in N.C.

A federal judge, of all people, recently upheld discrimination in a North Carolina voting law.

The regressive and restrictive law cuts out same-day

voter registration, pre-registration for 16- and 17-year-olds, cuts back on early voting by a week, bars counting votes outside voters' home precincts and requires voter ID.

Judge Thomas Schroeder, a Republican appointee, admitted the law was discriminatory to black voters. Yet he concluded--incredibly--"voting is no longer a problem in North Carolina and the law does not exacerbate existing disorders."

State lawmakers said the law was necessary to reduce voter fraud. Absurd. Voter fraud is infinitesimal. The law was really designed to reduce black voting. Blacks usually vote Democratic.

Enlightened Southern Governor

In sharp contrast, an enlightened Virginia governor issued an executive order restoring voting rights to more than 200,000 felons who have served their sentences.

Virginia had been one of just four states that kept felons from voting. (The others: Florida, Iowa and Kentucky.)

Gov. Terry McAuliffe wisely said in a statement: "I want you back in society. I want you feeling good about yourself. I want you voting, getting a job and paying taxes."

Governor McAuliffe is a Democrat. He served as chairman of the Democratic National Committee from 2001 to 2005.

He should run for president in 2020.

Restrictive Abortion Laws

South Carolina has become the 17th state banning abortion after 19 weeks. It, like the other anti-abortion states, faces challenges in the federal courts.

But South Carolina is undaunted, requiring abortion clinics to get admitting privileges for doctors and banning a second-trimester procedure known as an evacuation method. Exceptions: a mother's life is in danger a physician determines cannot survive.

Abortion is a mother's choice but the South Carolina primitives can only be deterred by the courts.

Oklahoma Makes Abortion a Felony

Another Southern state is even worse: the Oklahoma legislature passed a bill recently making abortion a felony. Doctors convicted under the law will be stripped of their medical licenses.

Republican state Senator Nathan Dahm explained the law: "Since I believe life begins at conception it should be protected. I also believe it's a core function of state government to defend that life from the moment of conception."

The Southern crackers are relentless in the assault on Roe v. Wade.

Sparks Tribune, Oct, 13, 2015

Garland bodes well for court

The recent appointment of Judge Merrick Garland to the Supreme Court could greatly change court rulings in a liberal direction.

Garland, chief judge of the U.S. Court of Appeals for the District of Columbia, is a centrist, having voted sometimes conservatively, sometimes liberally.

On the appeals court, he voted for Citizens United, the poisonous big money decision by the Supreme Court that illustrated its reactionary, pro-business, pro-corporation and anti-people rulings.

Garland sided with the government in cases involving habeas corpus petitions from detainees at Guantanamo Bay. He often voted against criminal defendants. He generally deferred to federal agencies.

That is why President Obama appointed him: Garland stands a better chance of being confirmed by a GOP-controlled Senate than an appointee with an ideological bent. He is widely acceptable to Republicans.

Senate majority leader Mitch McConnell insists there will be no confirmation hearings on Garland because lobbyists of the National Rifle Association told him so. But it is doubtful whether the Senate--even though ruled by the NRA--can fail to do its constitutional duty to confirm or deny an appointment.

Adam Liptak, New York Times Supreme Court reporter, praised Garland as "an able and modest judge" with a "meticulous work ethic and adherence to legal principles."

He described his legal career as prosecutor and judge as one displaying "fidelity to the Constitution and the law as cornerstones of his professional life." For instance, he has not objected to the death penalty, calling it "settled law."

In 19 years on the appeals court he dissented in just

16 cases, seeking rather to persuade the three-judge panels into consensus and unanimity.

He did that well. Justin Driver, University of Chicago law professor, noted: "He has long demonstrated an uncommon ability to find common ground among his fellow judges. That he manages to do so without sacrificing his core judicial principles is remarkable."

In his appeals court decisions, Judge Garland is often sympathetic to arguments of prosecutors yet he usually sided with unions. He upheld the National Labor Relations Board in 18 of 22 cases where employers committed unfair labor practices.

In a 2012 case he said his appeals court should accept the Drug Enforcement Agency assessment that marijuana is an illegal drug. "Don't we have to defer to their judgment?" he asked. "We're not scientists. They are." (DEA members are not scientists either.)

But Garland does not always defer to the government. He ruled for the Sierra Club in a case approving the Environmental Protection Agency's ozone Clean Air Act.

"We agree with the Sierra Club's principal contention that EPA was not authorized to grant conditional approval to plans that did nothing more than promise tomorrow what the act requires today," he wrote.

His impeccable resume began in West Niles High School from which he graduated in 1970. He was president of the student council, was on the debate team, acted in student theatrics and was voted the most intelligent male in his class.

Typical of his forward-looking attitude even as a youth, he spearheaded school committees that recommended eliminating final exams for graduating seniors and allowing shorts as acceptable school wear.

Garland, 63, son of Jewish immigrants, is a native of Skokie, Ill. Republicans and Democrats describe him as modest, thoughtful and moderate.

Garland graduated from Harvard Law School. While there he edited and wrote articles for The Harvard Law Review.

Perhaps most telling, he served as a clerk for William Brennan, the driving force behind the greatest Supreme Court in history, that of Chief Justice Earl Warren. Supreme Court members today call Garland a leading "feeder judge," sending more than 40 off his appeals court law clerks to work for the justices.

Garland's judicial philosophy calls for an independent judiciary. If he proves to be independent, he could be the crucial fifth vote halting the reactionary tide of the Supreme Court led by Chief Justice John Roberts.

Garland is a Democrat as a voter but nonpartisan as a judge. His stance is opposed to the five Republican justices that used to control the court. The Roberts Court was a Republican court despite Robert's threadbare argument claiming to be "just an umpire calling balls and strikes."

Two other Supreme Court appointees of President Obama, Justices Sonia Sotomayor and Elena Kagan, are firm liberals. Liberalism produces a far better court for most people and a much better nation.

Sparks Tribune, March 29, 2016

Social Issues

Clinton triumphs bode ill

Disastrous. Chaotic. Dysfunctional. Disorganized. Anachronistic. Fiasco. Embarrassing.

Those words describe the recent Nevada Democratic Party and Republican Party caucuses.

My wife and I spent a horrendous four and one-half hours waiting to get our choices registered for president in a Democratic caucus at a Reno precinct. With a primary we could have done it in 10 minutes.

A Reno resident complained in a letter to the Reno Gazette-Journal: "A caucus is a broken voting system. I set aside two hours to caucus for Bernie Sanders. I soon learned that it was going to take at least three hours. I left without my vote being counted or my voice being heard. Yet voting is a fundamental right we Americans have under the Constitution."

Another Reno resident wrote: "After seeing the disorganization and reading horror stories from around the state, I believe Nevada needs to return to a primary it dropped because it was costing the state too much money."

The writer is right. The Nevada caucus is such a "train wreck" that the only way to fix is to replace it with a primary--hang the cost.

At my precinct gathering room we constantly heard the message: "If you are in the wrong precinct go out to the registration desk." And still another constant message: "Wait, wait! Don't leave. We have more to do yet." Another constant announcement: "If you want to change your mind raise your hand."

It's inconceivable that more than a handful of Nevada caucus-goers would want to change their minds what with newspaper, TV, cable, radio and the Internet giving blanket coverage to campaigns--speeches, voting records and analysis of the candidates.

Waiting, waiting, waiting. So boring. In anguish, I

buried my head in my hands. Admittedly I don't have the patience of a saint but the endless delays and excuses were absurd. I shouted to my tablemates: "I'll never subject myself to this again."

Statements were exhaustively read for all candidates and the pros and cons of voting for each. Senator Sanders, a true revolutionary, proposed a $15 an hour minimum wage. In contrast, Hillary Clinton, a true middle-of-the roader, lacked specifics. She would just raise wages."

The Republican caucus reported computer problems and insufficient ballots in some precincts. One woman at Hug High School in Sparks said the precinct was supposed to open at 11:30 a.m. By 12:45 p.m. it was still closed.

At any rate, the real story of the caucus is the triumph of Clinton and how it bodes ill for the American people. To begin with, she is beholden to corporate power. She served on the corporate board of Walmart.

Women at Walmart are paid less than men. They advance to management at lower rates than men even though their performance reviews are higher. Clinton made no effort to combat this sexism. Walmart is vehemently anti-union while women make up the majority of workers. This is a woman-inequality issue she was silent about.

She rakes in $200,000 for most speaking engagements. She earned $11 million in 2014 for 51 speeches to banks and industries. She took in $675,000 for speeches to Goldman-Sachs.

The New York Times editorialized: " 'Everybody does it' is her mischievous-child defense for making closed-door, richly paid speeches to big banks but refusing to release transcripts. At candidate forums she gives a terrible answer: she'll release transcripts 'if everybody does it and that includes Republicans.'

"By stonewalling on transcripts Clinton suggests that she's not trustworthy and makes her own rules. Most important, she damages her credibility among Democrats who beg her to show them she'd run an accountable and transparent White House."

Clinton is called a liberal but she is centrist as nearly all presidents are, including the incumbent, Democratic President Obama. She is the same-old, same-old moderate like her husband, former President Bill Clinton.

Hawkish Record

She is an unabashed hawk. She supported the invasion of Iraq, the occupation and the counter-insurgency.

As secretary of state she backed an escalation of the Afghanistan war, pressed President Obama to arm Syrian rebels and endorsed airstrikes against the ruling Syrian regime. She supported intervention in Libya and lethal drone strikes.

As a U.S. senator from New York for eight years her record was doubly hawkish. She was the only Democratic senator who made false claims that Saddam Hussein gave sanctuary to Al-Qaeda..

Clinton has a dark legacy in the Mexican drug war, according to Jesse Franzblau in a foreign policy analysis for Truthout.

"U.S. law prohibits aid to nations guilty of human rights violations," he wrote. "Yet Clinton's state department regularly ignored widespread drug corruption and torture in Mexico."

Clinton opposes single-payer health care that Canada and most European nations happily have. Carl Bernstein writes that Clinton waged a battle to discredit Gennifer Flowers, an actress who had a long affair with Bill Clinton. H.C. dished her as "trailer trash."

Lisa Featherstone wrote in a Truthout op-ed piece: "Clinton's feminism is shallow. It is concerned with women at the top of our society while condoning abuse of those without power. It's not feminism. It's elitism."

President Clinton pushed the punitive crime bill

in 1994. Ms. Clinton supported it with an ugly remark: "They are not just gangs of kids anymore. They are super-predators."

By 1996 President Clinton's penal budget was twice the amount allocated to food stamps. He wanted "to end welfare as we know it." He railed against "welfare queens" and "big government." Mere nods from H.C.

Another indictment of a would-be president: the email controversy. While serving as secretary state Clinton used her family's private email server for official email communications rather than use proper State Departments accounts.

She destroyed 32,000 of those emails she deemed private, a clear violation of State Department rules and federal laws governing official recordkeeping. She destroyed them, declaring the emails personal and not work related.

Still another Clinton gambit while secretary of state that should bar her from being president: gifts to Saudi Arabia. She made weapons transfers to the Saudis a top priority while the Clinton Foundation accepted millions of dollars in donations from the Kingdom of Saudi Arabia and the weapons manufacturer Boeing.

"Despite the brutal attacks on Yemen and egregious domestic human rights violations, Saudi Arabia remains the number one U. S. ally in the Arab world," Medea Benjamin wrote in an op-ed for PINKtank.

"It's hard to exaggerate the enormity and high-tech nature of Saudi weapons purchases from the United States. The decade of 2010 constitutes the most enormous military sale in history. Weapons valued at $100 billion include F-15 bombers, Apache and Blackhawk helicopters, missiles, missile defense systems, bombs and armored vehicles."

Seeking to Prolong Dynasty

To sum up, the Clintons will use political influence,

money and connections to extend their dynasty for another tenure in the White House: Bill Clinton, the man from Hope, Ark., and Hillary Clinton, who hopes to become the first woman president. Her record shows she does not deserve it.

Another terrible caucus flaw that must be abolished is the proviso for Democratic super-delegates. Sanders carried Washoe County and tied Clinton in Nevada, 51 apiece. But because of the grossly unfair super-delegates, Clinton scored a 501 to 69 victory in Nevada.

Super-delegates are mostly establishment figures. They vote heavily for a status-quo figure like Clinton. In short, they make it impossible for Sanders to win the Democratic nomination for president.

On the Republican side, Donald Trump is in reach of the presidential nomination. Gov. Chris Christie of New Jersey smells a Trump triumph: he has already endorsed him.

This has stirred speculation that Christie will be a candidate for vice-president on a Trump ticket. Doubtful. Trump might better consider for his cabinet the blustery Christie as an obscure transportation secretary.

Sparks Tribune, March 8, 2016

Orlando once again shows
need for gun controls

The nation is mourning the recent massacre of 49 people at the gay Pulse nightclub in Orlando, Fla., the worst mass shooting in modern U.S. history.

The country also mourned after the senseless shooting murders at Charlestown, Aurora, Newtown, San Bernardino, Oak Creek, Chattanooga, Virginia Tech and Fort Hood.

Still, after repeated mass killings, Congress is unmoved. Members, mostly Republicans, listen to the commands of the National Rifle Association, not the demands of reason.

This violence level in the U.S. when measured against other countries is shameful. But Congress doesn't care.

Upshot magazine cites the gun homicide rate in Europe: just two people out of every million are shot to death by another person per year. So? the GOP asks.

About 300 million firearms are in private hands in the United States. You can go to a gun show at the local convention center and buy an assault rifle without a background check.

The New York Times published an editorial citing the factors behind the slaughter by Omar Mateen in Orlando:

"A virulent homophobia, a failure to identify and intercept those with a history of domestic abuse or threats of violence, and a radicalized strain of Islam that works daily to convert angry, disaffected people everywhere into mass killers."

Mateen's Domestic Abuse

As a perfect example of domestic abuse, Omar Mateen frequently beat his former wife, Sitora Yusufiy, confiscated her paychecks as a day-care teacher and isolated her in their Florida home. She fled in 2009 with the help of parents who took her back to their home in New Jersey. She justifiably got a divorce.

Yusufiy said six weeks after their marriage he began to behave erratically, flaring into temper tantrums without provocation and becoming verbally and physically abusive.

"Out of nowhere he would even abuse me when I was sleeping," she said. "He would make anti-gay comments when he was angry."

Islamic terrorist groups openly advertise America's lax gun laws to encourage those who want to carry out attacks here.

The Times gives the solutions:

"Washington's cowardly lawmakers have made these massacres easier by repeatedly refusing even to pass the most obvious and least burdensome measures like universal background checks, an assault weapons ban and empowering the FBI to block firearms sales to people on a terror-watch list."

Mateen slaughtered 49 people and wounded 53 with an assault rifle firing 30-round clips as fast as he could pull the trigger. Only the NRA has the insanity to endorse a weapon that no one should be allowed to carry.

The FBI, which investigated Mateen in 2013 and 2014 for suspected terrorist ties, may well have been stopped from purchasing guns if such laws had been enacted."

Strict gun controls will not stop all nefarious crimes by gun wielders but they will greatly reduce chances of deadly weapons getting into their hands.

Before the slaughter in Orlando, 95 percent of the deaths resulting from domestic terrorist attacks since 9/11 were inflicted by guns. Yet despite filibusters and sit-downs by Democratic senators, the Senate blocked four gun-control measures.

And as usual the retrograde U.S. Supreme Court sides with the NRA. In Heller v. District of Columbia in 2008, the court struck down a D.C. handgun ban, citing the Second Amendment.

NRA defenders and their ilk always cite the Second Amendment as a bulwark against any congressional gun laws: "A well regulated militia being necessary to the security of a free state, the right of the people to keep and bear arms shall not be infringed."

First, well regulated clearly means gun controls. Second, in the early days of the nation individual colonies (states) had militias, the equivalent of today's national guards, which are also well regulated.

Nevertheless, a federal appeals court judge, Maria Consuelo Callahan, dissented from a U.S. Ninth Circuit in San Francisco decision that found no right to carry concealed weapons.

Judge Callahan declared that "the Second Amendment grants protection to gun owners who carry concealed weapons. Like the rest of the Bill of Rights, this is part of the country's bedrock." Alas.

Europe's Generous Public Benefits

A recent article in The Nation magazine listed three countries in Europe and their "big benefits":

DENMARK: "The country is known for its superb record on gender equality, fostered through social-democratic programs--so much so that artist Roosh V wrote a book calling women too independent.

FRANCE: The French healthcare system offers universal coverage. It was ranked by the World Health Organization as the best in the world.

SWEDEN: College is free in Sweden, resulting in graduates with no crushing tuition-debt load. In the U.S. cumulative student debt is more than $1 trillion.

Sparks Tribune, June 28, 2016

Injustice Department

Criminal justice is not to be had under President Obama. As usual he talks big but acts small.

He recently visited El Reno, a medium security prison in Oklahoma, speaking passionately about the failings of a criminal justice system that has damaged a generation of Americans with far longer sentences than necessary.

So our noble president commuted the sentences of 46 prisoners serving 20 years for non-violent crimes, a piddling amount among 30,000 seeking clemency. This hardly lessens individual woes and U.S. costs of the huge prison population. The prison explosion was caused by the absurdity of mandatory minimum sentences for non-violent, low-level drug offenses.

Obama also complained at El Reno of intolerable conditions of 80,000 prisoners held in solitary confinement nationwide. He asked rhetorically: "Do we really think it makes sense to lock so many people alone in tiny cells for 23 hours a day, sometimes for months or even years?"

No. But Obama's Department of Injustice, as the New York Times calls it, has worked repeatedly behind the scenes for six years to make sure that tens of thousands of poor people--disproportionately minorities--languish in federal prison for what the courts have declared "illegal and unjustifiable" mandatory sentences.

"The case of Ezell Gilbert is emblematic of this injustice," the Times editorialized. "He was sentenced to nearly 25 years in prison for possession and intent to distribute 50 grams of crack cocaine. Even the sentencing judge called a quarter of century in prison far too harsh a sentence. Ten years later the Supreme Court confirmed that Gilbert's sentence was illegal."

Nevertheless, the Injustice Department convinced a federal judge from Florida that his two appeals were one more than allowed. The "finality" of criminal cases was too important, Obama's unjust bozos argued, even if clearly illegal. Fortunately, a federal appeals court rejected the administration's foolish argument, granting Gilbert freedom.

Human rights abuse OK

With all of that folly, Obama's administration finds it easy to send $1.3 billion worth of military aid to Egypt annually despite its frightful human rights abuses.

Sen. Patrick Leahy makes it clear a federal law he introduced bars military units that have committed atrocities from receiving U.S. aid.

The Obama government violates that law with impunity despite the custom of Cairo's security forces to kill demonstrators, murder people in custody and slaughter citizens during military operations in northern Sinai Peninsula.

The administration ignores the scorched-policy Egypt uses to fight militants everywhere.

Still more delay

Obama's efforts to shut down the Guantanamo Bay prison are collapsing--again. Clearly he is not trying hard enough. Three years ago national security officials concluded that the release of a prisoner held at Quantanamo did not pose a major risk.

Yet predictably, the Department of Injustice is fighting his release. Ashton Carter in his first seven months as defense secretary has yet to make a decision on Obama's resolve. Carter's delay echoes that of his predecessor, Chuck Hagel.

The administration, with its great resolution, is now holding cabinet-level "principles committee" meetings discussing how to close Guantanamo before the president leaves office in 15 months. (Want to bet it's still open when Obama leaves office?)

No one heeds retired Supreme Court Justice John Paul Stevens anymore. But his May speech was wise: "Onerous provisions have hindered the president's ability to close Guantanamo," he said. "They make no sense and have no precedent in history. Congress's actions are even more irrational than the detention of Japanese-Americans during World War II."

Broad powers of the anti-terrorist act of 9/11 are used to wage perpetual war against al-Qaeda. They are wielded as Obama's legal rationale for holding people prisoners indefinitely.

Charge them or release them. There is no reason to hold someone in prison for 13 years without charge.

After reopening the Cuban embassy in Washington, D.C., Cuban foreign minister Bruno Rodriguez rightly declared that the United States must hand back Guantanamo Bay at once. And so it must.

As Rodriguez says: "Removal of the economic, commercial and financial blockade causes so much deprivation and damage to our people. The return of occupied territory in Guantanamo and respect for the sovereignty of Cuba is essential."

True. But the U.S. has respect only for what it desires.

Cold War still exists

Okinawa, the smallest of Japan's 47 prefectures, is occupied by 32 foreign powers including America. About 75 percent of the military bases are American. The Cold War never ended for Okinawans.

Why are the 1.4 million people of Okinawa continually saddled with the burden of the Japanese government? Okinawa is Japan's prime military staging ground. Politics rules whether in Japan or America.

Sparks Tribune, Sept. 8, 2015

The IS kills in guise of religion

Not Islamic and not a state but a murderous death cult.

Heading on a cartoon in The Guardian of Britain showing a hooded, grinning skeleton of an IS killer carrying a rifle and sword.

Terrorism abroad and in America by murderous jihadists has some pundits, politicians and presidential candidates calling for war.

But war is not the answer to the Islamic State (IS). As Nation magazine declared recently: "Talk of fighting a war against criminals bestows on them a dignity their despicable killings do not warrant. It merely covers them with undeserved glory."

While not at war, drone strikes at IS positions show the seriousness of U.S. opposition to the warlike and grossly irreligious group. The IS is an organized crime ring.

It massacres innocent people in Europe and America, seizes territory in Syria and Iraq, enacts taxes and tolls on people in conquered lands. This leads to paying smugglers for protection. In Syria the terrorists closed a hospital because so many doctors fled in fear.

The IS beheads foes. It holds a journalist for 10 months seeking ransom. It enjoys killing. One jihadist says: "It is pleasant to see the blood of disbelievers flow...I rely on Allah while killing European and American disbelievers."

Reactionary Saudi Arabia supports the extremist jihadists financially and by spreading its vicous doctrines in Koranic schools, mosques and among clerics.

Analyst Noam Chomsky describes Turkey's phony "war" on terrorism as "one of the most hypocritical gestures in the annals of diplomacy." No wonder Russian President Vladimir Putin called Turkey "accomplices of terrorists" for downing a Russian jet fighter.

In America, gun massacres have erupted in California,

Colorado, Connecticut, Oregon and South Carolina. After each one, outraged cries fill newspapers, airways and social media. Yet after each one a reactionary Congress remains adamant: no gun controls.

Europeans are astonished that Congress backs the notorious National Rifle Association, calling deaths from homicides in the Western world "as rare as deaths from falling tree limbs or plane crashes."

But the majority of congressional politicians are beholden to the NRA for their campaign money. To Congress, money trumps repeated massacres. Congress will not even consider expanding background checks and denying gun purchases to terrorists on the government's no-fly list.

California has the toughest gun-safety law in the nation. But it is not tough enough as the recent San Bernardino, Calif., massacre proved.

The two attackers there had Smith & Wesson and Panther Arms assault rifles. Those are military and police weapons. They should be outlawed for private citizens.

"It is a moral outrage and a national disgrace that people can legally purchase weapons designed to kill with brutal speed and efficiency," The New York Times editorialized. "They are weapons of war, marketed as tools of macho vigilantism and even insurrection."

The San Bernardino terrorists, Syed Rizwan Farook, 28, and his wife, Tashfeen Mank, 29, killed 14 people and wounded 22 others in the Inland Regional Center for treating disabilities. They fired 75 bullets in the center and 75 more in the police shootout that killed them.

An ironic religious note: Farook presented himself to her on an online Muslim dating site as a devout Muslim memorizing the Quran. He grew up in southern California. She was born in Pakistan and sometimes lived in Saudi Arabia.

They married and lived in a comfortable suburban home

near San Bernardino. All the comforts of home included a huge arms stockpile: 2,500 rounds for automatic rifles, 2,000 rounds for pistols and 12 pipe bombs.

After every massacre politicians offer prayers but nothing useful like reforming the puny U.S. gun laws.

Feminist Revolution in Syria

Amid the misery of war-torn Syria, the northern Kurdish region of Rojava is witnessing a democratic and humanist revolution centering on ethnic minorities and women.

It is a profound experiment in grassroots, participatory democracy, Tony Iltis and Stuart Munckton reported in an op-ed article for the online teleSUR.

"The emphasis on women's liberation is reflected in the high visibility of women fighters in Rojava's revolutionary armed groups," Iltis and Munckton declare.

The Rojavan revolution received much attention through the heroic resistance by the freedom fighters of the People's Protection Units and Women's Protection Units in defeating an Islamic State siege on the Rojavan town of Kobane earlier this year.

Women's councils exist at all levels of government: the commune, the district, the city and the canton. Women have veto power on all issues concerning women.

Rojava is now a "liberated zone" in the Kurdistan area. The major political party is the Democratic Union, which is aligned with the Turkish left-wing Kurdish Workers Party.

Sparks Tribune Dec. 15, 2015

Ban trophy hunting

Trophy hunting is dreadful whether it occurs in the United States or the rest of the world. It should be banned everywhere.

The worldwide outrage over the killing of Cecil, beloved lion of Zimbabwe citizens, was justified. Trophy hunting is inhumane. It is unsportsmanlike.

The case of Cecil is particularly abhorrent. An American trophy hunter lured him to his death from Zimbabwe's Hwange National Park. The culprit: Walter Palmer, a dentist from Bloomington, Minn.

Cecil, a tourist attraction and subject of research by academics at Oxford University, was wounded by a bow and arrow shot by Palmer. Then he lured the lion out of the park with bait. Palmer tracked Cecil for 40 hours before fatally shooting him with a gun.

Palmer had the head severed, intending to take it home as a trophy until thwarted by Zimbabwe officials.

This is hardly sport. He should be extradited to Zimbabwe for a criminal trial.

A sign posted on the door of Palmer's dental office read: "Rot in hell." One demonstrator outside his office screamed into a megaphone: "Murderer! Terrorist!"

Palmer apologized as people usually do after a dreadful deed or having uttered a racist slur. Apologies are wasting newspaper space. They can't bring back the dead or erase the racism. Palmer went into hiding in shame and became the center of a firestorm over the ethics of trophy hunting.

Trophy hunting is undertaken by the obscenely wealthy who pay tens of thousands to kill protected animals. A Texas man once paid $350,000 to hunt and kill a rhino in Namibia. Palmer paid $50,000 to kill Cecil, a 13-year-old lion with a jet black mane.

Social media stirred world outrage. However, the old-fashioned newspaper letter is better written, longer, more thoughtful and even philosophical. Take this letter to the San Francisco Chronicle from James Blackman of San Francisco:

"The lion represents pride, family, majestic beauty, a creature to both fear and admire. The lion embodies everything America holds dear--at a distance. He is a symbol of the great wild that once was. The death of Cecil represents the vast capitalistic destruction of that wild."

Richard Conniff is the author of "The Species Seekers: Heroes, Fools and the Mad Pursuit of Life on Earth." Conniff is a hero. He is a trophy hunter with a great difference: he shoots with a camera. His subject: black rhinos in Namibia.

Trophy hunters kill rhinos and elephants to sell their lucrative horns. They are what Conniff calls "coldhearted, soulless zombies, criminal gangs driven by perverse consumer appetite." To him, rhinos are magnificent animals, like ancient triceratops come back to life.

Another perversity: collecting shark fins. As of 2012, Truthout reports that 70 million sharks were killed worldwide just for their fins.

"If there is one single entity that's allowing this disturbing business to continue, it's shipping giant UPS," Kevin Matthews laments in a Truthout op-ed.

About 5,000 black rhinos survive this cruel world. Namibia, twice the size of California, has organized communal conservancies of rhinos to guard them from poachers. Black ranchers and herders run them.

Several members of Congress have introduced a bill to halt importation of lion trophies. Major airlines no longer carry big-game trophies as cargo. Some include Delta, American, United Airlines, Air France, KLM and Qantas.

USA Today editorialized: "Trophy hunting is pointless. The most prolific hunters are Americans who in 2013 imported 292 wild lion trophies. Hunters are wooed by promises of thrills and luxuries such as sumptuous pools and spas. Hunters can employ four-wheel-drive vehicles and animal baiting."

Four-wheel drives! What noble hunters.

The Wall Street Journal weighed in on the issue, noting that the wild African lion population has declined 42 percent over the past 20 years to fewer than 20,000. Meanwhile, Africa's human population is the fastest growing in the world.

"In roughly the same period as the lion decline, the number of Africans has nearly doubled to 1.2 billion. African people are developing more and more suburbs and thus encroaching more and more on the territory of lions."

Personally, even domestic hunting is troublng. I have never forgotten a Reader's Digest account of a deer hunt by a father and his young son I read 70 years ago.

They were having no luck until the father glimpsed a deer in the distance. He instructed his son to stand still while he circled around and drove the deer toward him.

Just as he planned, the father succeeded. When the deer loomed right in front of the boy, the youth gazed in admiration--and slowly lowered his rifle. When his dad rushed up, he asked why he didn't shoot the deer that stood right in front of him.

"It was too beautiful to kill," he replied.

The father, instead of being angry, gently said: "My son, you have learned compassion."

Sparks Tribune, Aug. 18, 2015

Weekly outrage, cheers and jeers

British actor Benedict Cumberbatch rightly detests cellphones and cameras being punched and flashed while he is acting. The Digital Age has long since become the Insensitive and Discourteous Age.

During his recent performance of "Hamlet" at the Barbican in London, Cumberbatch was about to deliver the "To be or not to be" soliloquy when a red light flashed from the third row.

"It's mortifying," he said. "There is nothing less supportable or enjoyable."

The Barbican promptly installed devices that can detect phones and cameras during performances. Offenders will be evicted immediately.

The theater should go even further, barring cellphones and cameras. If insensitive people can't exist for a couple of hours without the evils of modernity, they shouldn't be allowed to spoil play–going for those who can.

Righto Sanders

Sen. Bernie Sanders of Vermont, Democratic candidate for president, would make tuition free for all undergraduates at public universities and colleges. Righto!

The federal government could easily pay for it just by slashing military funding. Let's have fewer wars and more social benefits from Congress.

Students and their families are going deeper into debt. The average debt after four years is $25,600. The interest rate is so exorbitant they will spend half their lives paying it off.

It hardly needs saying that more college-educated men and women will greatly improve society and aid the economy.

Larry Schwartz, in an AlterNet op-ed, wrote: "Most developed countries are appalled at the idea of burdening young people with debt for a college education and strengthening the nation. In countries like Germany, Brazil, Norway, Iceland and even Panama, public university tuition is free."

Bogus voter fraud

The New York Times reports that "many people, including the Supreme Court, have bought into the fallacious line about voter fraud. It does not exist. The real voter fraud is the Texas ID law.

Such laws are racially discriminatory and anti-voter schemes. A federal appeals court panel recently ruled unanimously that the Texas ID law had a harmful effect on black and Latino voters and therefore violates the 1965 Voting Rights Act.

Another example of how federal courts so often make sure all people are granted liberty.

Climate change gains

President Obama's clean power plan has an answer to people who reject climate change, imposing nationwide limits on carbon-dioxide pollution from power plants. These plants are the source of 31 percent of America's greenhouse gas emissions.

"It will shut down hundreds of coal-fired power plants and give momentum to carbon-free energy sources like wind and solar power," the Times editorialized. "Having already set fuel efficiency standards for cars and trucks, Obama now has leverage with other nations heading into the United Nations climate-change conference in December in Paris."

Opposition to clean power comes, as expected, from the industry, Congress and the states.

Pot backing grows

Obama has the "slows" when it comes to urging

marijuana prohibition. Pot is classified as a Schedule I drug like heroin and LSD under the Controlled Substances Act.

The absurdity is manifest. Pot is an important medical need for some people. Moreover, it is no more harmful than too much alcohol. It should be removed from the prohibited list.

Four states and the District of Columbia have already made recreational use of pot legal: Alaska, Colorado, Oregon and Washington. Nevadans and Ohioans are expected to vote for legalization next year and Californians in 2017.

While Obama and Congress balk, a few states are leading the so-called leader.

Pentagon wars on journalists

The Defense Department recently released a manual outlining its interpretation of the laws of war. A hefty 1,176-page document, few Americans are likely to read it.

The Times in an editorial "reads" it for us: "The manual outlines the treatment of journalists covering armed conflicts that would make their work more dangerous, cumbersome and subject to censorship. These provisions should be repealed immediately.

"Allowing this document to stand as guidance for commanders, government lawyers and officials of other nations would do severe damage to press freedom. Authoritarian rulers around the world could point to it to show that their despotic treatment of journalists--including Americans--is in line with the standards set by the U.S. government."

Journalists are usually regarded as civilians but in the jargon of the Pentagon sometimes "unprivileged belligerents." This means they are sometimes afforded fewer protections than war combatants.

The manual ominously warns: "Reporting on military operations can be similar to collecting intelligence--or even spying."

So the military now spies on civilians and journalists.

Cuba still the enemy

The U.S. and Cuba are restoring relations. Good. Now Congress should promptly repeal the dreadful embargo and cruel sanctions.

A half-century of hostility to and coercion of Cuba not only failed to topple the Castro regime but showed how ruthless and merciless America can be.

Sparks Tribune, Aug. 25, 2015

Get police out of schools

It's long past the time when police officers are removed from schools. They do more harm than good.

"Abundant research shows that having cops in schools does nothing to reduce crime," Nation magazine reported. "Instead, police create an atmosphere of fear and intimidation resulting in the criminalization of young people of color."

The New York Times estimated that more that 17,000 police officers are posted in schools. Twenty-eight percent of all schools have armed security officers.

Ever since the Columbine, Colorado, school massacre in 1999, armed police in schools became commonplace. But the real problems in schools--bullying, mental illness and the widespread availability of guns--have been scantily dealt with.

The Nation continued: "Schools with high percentages of black and Latino students are more likely to have zero-tolerance policies resulting in more suspensions, expulsions and arrests. Even more disturbing, school police are using a high level of physical force."

One of many terrible examples: a white police officer, Ben Field, slammed a 16-year-old black student to the floor in her South Carolina classroom in October, breaking her arm. Fields faces a federal lawsuit accusing him of "recklessly targeting African-American students."

Another case: a 17-year-old student in Texas in 2014 was Tasered by a "school resource officer" (SRO) while the youth was trying to break up a school fight. The student was critically injured in the Taser fall and subsequent blow from the SRO. The kid spent 52 days in a coma. A surveillance video showed he was actually stepping away from the SRO.

Another example of many similar SRO abuses: 14-year-old, Derek Lopez, was shot to death in 2014 by an

SRO in San Antonio, Texas, after he punched a student on school grounds. Officer Daniel Alvarado ordered the boy to freeze, chased him to a shed and killed him.

The Houston Chronicle reported that in the last four years Houston-area school districts reported 1,300 cases of SRO use of force.

Argument proved. As the Supreme Court ruled in Tinker v. Des Moines (1969), students do not "shed their constitutional rights at the school house gate."

Yet the Obama administration has called for an additional $15 million to add 1,000 more school resource officers. Moreover, the administration wants the Justice Department to develop "a model of the best practices" for using SROs.

There never will be a model SRO practice. The worst practices are already evident. Police simply don't belong in schools.

Don't Donate to Fat Cats

The very names prompt tender feelings about Christmas donations: United Nations Children's Fund, The American Red Cross, the March of Dimes and Goodwill. But think again before you donate to them at yuletide or any other tide.

Marsha Evans, Red Cross CEO, makes $650,000 in yearly salary plus expenses. The March of Dimes gives away just 10 cents of every charitable dollar received. Caryl Stern, the CEO of UNICEF, reaps $1,200,000 a year plus expenses and a Rolls Royce. Less than five cents a dollar goes to charity.

Goodwill owner and CEO Mark Curran bags $2.3 million a year for good items given free to Goodwill. United Way President nabs $375,000 a year along with numerous expense benefits.

These staggering figures come from a highly reliable source: James Spangler, public watchdog extraordinaire who monitors charities. Spangler recommends giving to Salvation Army and Doctors Without Borders as the best charitable organizations because most of the donations to them actually reach the needy.

Down with Monarchy

Jeremy Corbyn, rabid republican who is the leftist leader of the British Labor Party, refused to sing "God Save the Queen" at a recent Buckingham Palace ceremony. He also refused to speak to Queen Elizabeth II on bended knee.

Traditionalists were shocked. Apparently they never heard of the French Revolution.

The monarchy is not just centuries obsolete, it costs millions to the few nations that still have them. They are used merely for pomp and circumstance to please crowds. Sensible nations have long since shed such antiquities.

Principle Before Glory

Patricia Canning Todd, who died recently, was one of the long forgotten pioneers of the women's liberation movement.

She won four tennis Grand Slam singles titles in 1947 and 1948 but gave up a chance to win a fifth in 1948 when she refused to play in the French Open final because the match was relegated to a side court.

"Todd played relentlessly, using a devilish backhand to beat such stars as Gussie Moran and Louise Brough," a New York Times obit reported. She was 93.

Sparks Tribune, Dec. 1, 2015

British rightly vote to leave European Union

Despite doomsayers and forecasters of disaster if Great Britain cut ties with the European Union, the British voters wisely choose to leave the union.

"One of the good things about Brexit is the rich curriculum of lessons it offers leaders and electorates in other democratic countries," Washington Post columnist E.J. Dionne wrote. "Citizens who live in the economically ailing peripheries of wealthy nations are in revolt against well-off and cosmopolitan metropolitan areas.

"Older voters lock in decisions that young voters reject. Traditional political parties on the Left and Right are being torn asunder. Areas usually voting heavily for Labor candidates cried 'enough' of happy and prosperous London." (Londoners voted overwhelmingly to stay in the EU.)"

As the New York Times editorialized: "A gamble on the unknown was better than staying with the present over which they had no control. It was a cry of anger and frustration from a class that felt alienated from those who wield power, wealth and privilege both in the British government and Brussels, the EU capital. It was a world they felt was leaving them out."

Populist anger at the established order had finally boiled over. The Brits had rebelled. The vote was a rebuke to the establishment. As Fraser Nelson, England's Daily Telegraph columnist, said: "It was the biggest slap in the face ever delivered to the British establishment in the history of universal suffrage."

British voters were tired of rule by and for the elites.

The idea of a 28-nation common defense has always been nonsensical in a nuclear age. As for its free-trade provisions, Donald Trump rightly blistered the Trans-Pacific Partnership (TPP), calling it rape of the U.S. economy.

Free trade sounds great but would cost scores of American jobs as already seen in outsourcing that swells corporation profits but harms workers. If elected president, eurosceptic Trump promised to withdraw from TPP--if it is ever enacted by Congress. In his plea to restore U.S. economic independence, he denounced China's currency devaluation in order to take advantage of the U.S. monetary system.

Small is Better

So the sun is again setting on the British Empire, pleasing Matthew d'Ancona, political columnist for the UK's The Guardian who says "small is beautiful."

Farewell to Shakespeare's rhapsodic words in "Richard II": "This sceptered isle, this demi-paradise, this happy breed of men, this blessed plot, this earth, this England" (Act 2, Scene I). Great Britain has become Little England.

Withdrawal was an astounding decision, resulting in political turmoil, volatile global stock markets and gyrations in worldwide currency markets. (The British pound fell to a 31-year low after the Brexit vote.)

The Leave vote also again encouraged other nations yearning to be free. It revived independence movements in Scotland, Northern Ireland and Wales, which deserve to be free of Britain's shackles. The 300-year-old UK is threatened.

In Spain, the Catalan independence movement yearns for freedom from the reign of Spain and the rule of France.

In France, Marine Le Pen, president of the National Front Party, called the Brexit vote "an act of courage of people who embrace their freedom." She asked in a column printed by the New York Times: "Do we want an undemocratic authority ruling our lives? No!

"In the name of ideology, different countries are forced to adopt the same currency. It's ridiculous that a Polish member of the European Parliament makes law for Spain.

France and The Netherlands they rightly voted against the EU constitution. The Greeks correctly revolted against a Brussels-imposed austerity plan.

The British vote for withdrawal is the People speaking.

Cameron's Austerity Despised

The exit voters shattered the Conservative Party and its prime minster, David Cameron, who staked his office on a no-vote. The working class is rightly furious about Cameron's austerity government and feel neglected.

His conservatism never suited Britain, far more suited to Left Labor--and not the sell-out variety of former Laborite prime minister Tony Blair.

The resignation of Cameron paves the way for a Laborite to become prime minister of England. A Labor leader should restore the luster of the once glorious Labor Party which brought the country universal health care.

Yves Smith, author and financial expert, declared that the EU has broken down. It has, she said, "ceased to satisfy its citizens' needs and aspirations. It is heading for a disorderly disintegration." (It costs the British government about $175 million a year in dues.)

Brexit is an awfully complicated matter what with Article 50 and other arcane matters. But withdrawal from the EU promises a brighter day for the English people.

Sparks Tribune, July 5, 2016

Scams bedevil the unwary

This column, although it tells about my wife's horrifying experience, is not just about her. It is a column designed to alert the unwary of the costly price of being duped.

Here's what happened to her:

"I recently received a phone call from a Florida number (305-600-3299)," she said. "The male voice called me grandma and I responded, 'Doug'? 'Yes,' he replied.

"He said he was in Miami for a friend's funeral and had been jailed for a traffic accident, running a red light and knocking over a pregnant woman. Then a purported lawyer, "David Ross," called saying my grandson needed $950 bail money plus a $50 charge.

"He told me to go to the nearest Western Union and mail the money to Martha Blakney, a supposed bondswoman from New Jersey. Terribly concerned and upset, I went to my bank and withdrew $1,000.

"The Western Union clerk suspected a scam but I did not believe her. However, one other person in the office was familiar with arrests. He convinced me it was a fraud because of incorrect bail procedure.

"I phoned my grandson and was relieved to learn he was safe--400 miles from Miami. I was also happy to save $1,000 that my stupidity could have cost me."

"I later Googled the telephone number (a land line) and a street photo showed a house with two late-model vehicles in the driveway."

A friend sent my wife an email saying she knows people "who fall for this one." One of her friends recently was scammed by an email from a friend "stranded overseas." My wife's friend admitted that even her intelligent husband was victimized by a similar scheme.

"They are ingenious and make me so mad," my wife's

friend lamented. "There are places you can report them but it is very hard to catch them."

So my wife did not bother reporting her case.

This scam is so often successful because family members have a powerful urge to help another family member in trouble.

Virginity Tests

Privacy is of no concern to the Afghanistan government warped by many bogus religious beliefs.

The Afghanistan Human Rights Commission recently reported from Kabul that women and girls in jails are frequently subjected to forced virginity tests. It denounced the "discredited practice" and called for an end to the "invasive and degrading practice."

The New York Times reported that female detainees across 12 of the country's 34 provinces were interviewed. Some of those victimized were girls, many as young as 13.

"Moreover, the procedure is frequently conducted in the presence of many people in an invasive manner that amounts to rape or torture," the Times declared.

A letter writer to the Times, Widney Brown, director of Physicians for Human Rights in New York City, called virginity tests "a form of sexual violence masquerading as science."

"Health professionals who conduct these exams are violating the ethical duty to do no harm," Brown said. "Both the European Court of Human Rights and the Inter-American Court of Human Rights have held that forced virginity tests constitute torture."

The 750 women in Afghanistan jails and prisons are being held on such vague charges as committing "moral crimes."

Moral crimes? Running away from home either with a lover other than the husband arranged for them by their families or for escaping domestic violence.

Afghanistan is a long, long way from being civilized.

No Class

A sports columnist for the San Francisco Chronicle used a stuffy academic word, iteration, in the first paragraph of her column. I read no farther.

I sent her an email saying it is not a word used by sports writers with simplicity, grace and class. Instead of emailing back her disagreement, she emailed this insulting reply: "What kind of third-rate college did you go to?"

The other day in an Associated Press soccer story I read that a team "replicated" an earlier victory. Replicated means the same as iteration. Repeat or repeating in both instances would be far better words to use.

Another example of lack of class: a Reno editor, with whom I frequently exchanged emails about possible cover stories, sent his rejection of my recent article on the late Justice Scalia via an email from his sub-editor.

People Power

I wrote to the sports editor of the Reno Gazette-Journal suggesting that I was probably the only one of his readers who noticed or cared that the daily listing of sports events on TV was eliminated. I explained that I had cut out the listings for decades.

He wrote back that I wasn't the only one. Fifty other people sent him emails saying they miss the listings. Under such pressure, the publisher of the paper restored the item. Sometimes publishers do listen to complaints of readers.

Sparks Tribune, March 15, 2016

Terrorism of Blacks

The past is never dead. It's not even past.
Faulkner, "Requiem for a Nun" (1951)

The media rightly call it terrorism when the Islamic State kills people. The media now should begin calling it terrorism when whites slaughter African Americans.

The white-hooded KKK bombed the 16th Street Baptist Church in Birmingham, Alabama, in 1963, killing four little black girls and injuring 20.

Alexander Stephens, Confederate vice-president, proclaimed in a 1861 speech: "The confederacy rests on the great truth that the negro is not equal to the white man, that slavery, subordination to the superior race, is his natural condition."

Nothing has changed about the essence of that speech 144 years ago and the recent terrorist bombing of the Emanuel African Episcopal Methodist Church in Charlestown, S.C. A white terrorist murdered nine unarmed blacks there, continuing the never-ending theme of white-supremacy killing.

Black killings have echoed recently in Ferguson, Mo., Baltimore, Md., Brooklyn, N.Y., and Cleveland, Ohio. Trayvon Martin of Miami Gardens, Fla., was slain by George Zimmerman, a Neighborhood Watch terrorist. Killing of blacks, young and old, never ceases.

The whole American system, way of life and philosophy encourage this terrorism.

President Obama, eulogizing the Charlestown victims, sang the opening refrain of "Amazing Grace" on national television. Fine. But that will hardly end the terrorism. The promise of the Declaration of Independence ("that all men are created equal') does not apply to blacks.

Emanuel parishioners immediately called for healing, days of mourning, peace marches and national prayers.

Decent sentiments. But none of these steps will cure the problem.

Danish philosopher Thomas Brudholm points out in his book, "Resentment's Virtue," that advocacy of healing "fetishizes forgiveness and reconciliation." He shows how negative emotions are not only understandable in the aftermath of a mass atrocity but that they possess a moral component often ignored by boosters of reconciliation."

No wonder an angry black woman told her Twitter circle: "She refuses to heal, refuses to participate in a system of structural racism and refuses to acquiesce in the norms of white people. Calls for healing and a return to normalcy are calls to stop crying about the deadly effects of white supremacy."

Another woman wrote that she was angered by calls not to be angry. "I am angry at the entrenched system of white supremacy and the duplicitous vocabulary being used to discuss the Charlestown massacre," she said. "Calls for healing, injunctions against anger and the theme of a lone-wolf killer, Emanuel slayer Dylann Roof, are complicit with right-wing attempts to maintain the racial status quo."

One writer after the Emanuel slaughter recalled Obama and Martin Luther King quoting Theodore Parker, Unitarian church preacher and abolitionist: "The arc of the moral compass is long but it bends toward justice." Unfortunately for blacks, it does not.

Another American pathology fosters the killings: lack of gun controls and the ease of obtaining guns. The Supreme Court wrongly calls gun controls unconstitutional under a wrong interpretation of the Second Amendment ("the right of the people to keep and bear arms").

Congress could enact strong gun controls but it will not because too many voters cherish their guns.

Simple proposals like background checks for gun sales could not get enacted in Congress even after the massacre of 20 children in Sandy Hook, Conn. Congress remained unmoved by nine black men and women shot dead by a white man during a Bible study class.

Obama rightly notes: "You don't see murder on this scale and frequency in any other advanced nation on earth." True. The United States is not a civilized country.

Racism, murder and terrorism of blacks never end.

Slavery symbol banished

Alabama Gov. George Wallace proclaimed infamously in 1963: "segregation now, segregation tomorrow and segregation forever." Almost.

Not until last week, following the Emanuel turmoil, did South Carolina banish the Confederate flag from state capitol grounds in Columbia, S.C. Not until two weeks ago did the Citadel, 173-year-old South Carolina military school in Columbia, remove the Confederate Naval Jack from the campus chapel.

Yes, many Southerners hold the Confederate flag in reverence because their ancestors carried the banner into battle. Statues, memorials and roadside markers of Confederate President Jefferson Davis dot the South. Incredibly, a bronze of Davis stands in the U.S. Capitol.

But blacks have a far better argument: it is an insult to memorialize symbols of slavery. (In 1860 one in three people in the South owned slaves as property worth $3 billion. Confederate President Jefferson Davis admitted that slavery was indispensable to the Southern economy.)

Weldon Hammond, a black South Carolinian who fought desegregation in the early 1960s, called the Confederate flag "something that for all their lives blacks have been trying to disinherit."

Yet Texas, until its law was recently struck down by the U.S. Supreme Court, would have made the Confederate flag one of its specialty license plates. The Confederate flag is finally being consigned to historic relic rooms.

Sparks Tribune, July 14, 2015

Bleak prospects for trade accord

The huge multinational trade deal, the Trans-Pacific Partnership (TPP), is being thoroughly trashed in this year's campaigning for president, leading some political observers to doubt it will ever be signed by Congress.

A news analysis by Ian Gustafson of the Council on Hemispheric Affairs reported that the United States has exerted "extraordinary influence" over the agreement. He declared:

"Though the TPP is presented as a disinterested effort to stimulate economic growth in the Pacific Rim, it serves to advance the world's leading corporations."

President Obama is promoting the 12-nation trade agreement, signed last October. However, Sen. Bernie Sanders, a Democratic presidential candidate from Vermont, disagreed with his party leader. He noted what he calls the devastation of U.S. trade accords.

"Since 2001 we have lost 60,000 factories and five million decent-paying manufacturing jobs," he reports. "We must end our disastrous trade policies. You cannot pass a trade bill like TPP that sends jobs out of our country so that companies here can break unions, force down wages and trim benefits for already wealthy Wall Street executives and investors."

Sanders cited other the miserable trade pacts: North American Free Trade Agreement (NAFTA), Central American Free Trade Agreement (CAFTA) and Permanent Normal Trades Relations (PNTR). In short, the devastation of U.S. trade accords.

Obama put TPP on a "fast track" so the American people could not digest, debate and learn what commentators said about this "fast" scam.

Jim Hightower, a true populist in an age when every politician claims the mantle of populism, is blunt about

68

TPP: "A cabal of global corporations and their friends in the Obama administration waged a wholesale assault on jobs, health, the environment and people's sovereignty."

Moreover, Hightower declared that the trade pact worked out in secret uses "wonkish, gibberistic jargon to mask a corporate boondoggle--the largest trade flimflam in history--negotiated by corporate lobbyists and government lawyers."

The vital interests of the American people render secrecy anathema. Or, as economist Robert Reich put it: "When corporations, Wall Street and the wealthy get special goodies, the rest of us get shafted. The TPP is being sold as a way to boost the U.S. economy, expand exports and contain China's widening economic influence. "

In fact, it's just more "trickle-down economics." It gives big corporations and Wall Street a way to eliminate any laws and regulations that get in the way of their profits."

Meanwhile, here's the way the tragic deal works: "Massachusetts-based New Balance is already struggling to make its athletic shoes profitable because of cheap imports. TPP removes tariffs from Vietnamese and Malaysian shoes, benefitting Nike and greatly undermining New Balance."

Other woes of the trade scheme: it gives Big Pharma a virtual patent monopoly. Dean Baker, writing for Truthout, noted: "The Hepatitis-C drug Solvaldi sells for $84,000 a treatment in its patent-protected version in the United States. But a high-quality generic version is available in India for $1,000."

Diane Archer, in an op-edit column for Truthout, says that the hush-hush TPP contains a startling provision: "a Medicare poison pill."

"The bill includes $700 million in Medicare cuts at the end of a 10-year budget period to cover the cost of trade adjustment assistance for displaced workers, Americans who will lose their jobs because of low-cost imports," she writes.

Obama complained that his Democratic "fellow travelers on progressive issues were 'whupping on' him about trade policy." But as Nation magazine pointed out:

"Obama's dismissal of concerns about TPP undermines his credibility. First, he was unwilling to declassify the text of an agreement that was negotiated behind closed doors with input from corporations which supported it enthusiastically. Second, Obama's suggestion that opponents were just 'making stuff up' denies the experience and insight of progressive critics of free-trade absolutism."

The mainstream media usually dismiss trade accords as arcane stuff of little news value. The truth is otherwise. Doctors Without Borders declared that TPP "will go down in history as the worst trade agreement for access to medicines in developing countries."

It predicts that half a billion people will be deprived of medicines if TPP takes effect. Yet Obama continues to push a loser. Dean Baker, in a Truthout op-ed, observed that the real story of TTP is that "it has little to do with trade."

"The United States already has trade deals with six of the 12 participating nations," Baker pointed out. "Moreover, TPP puts into question every health, safety and environmental regulation in America."

The opposition coalition of unions, environmentalist groups and public advocacy groups resisting global trade agreements is powerful. President Obama will have a tough time persuading Congress to back the pact.

If passed. That is the key question. It certainly appears that Congress will not approve TPP, doing the right thing for a change.

Yet Obama continues to push a loser.

Robert Reich, former head of the Labor Department, called it "The largest, most disastrous trade deal you've never heard of. It gives big corporations and Wall Street a way to eliminate any laws and regulations that get in the way of their profits."

Baker, in the Truthout op-ed, observed that the real story of TTP is that "it has little to do with trade."

Sparks Tribune, April 12, 2016

Secret trade scam denounced

President Obama is first in war and last in peaceful trade pacts.

Everyone knows he is a warmonger. Few know he is an exponent of worldwide trade deals that do colossal harm to the American people.

The House of Representatives recently voted, 218-208, for Obama's trade pact for the One Percent. The bill went to the Senate where horse-trading saved Obama's disaster. The far wiser majority of Democrats, defying their president, voted en masse against the bill.

The accord, the 12-country Trans-Pacific Partnership (TPP), does nothing for U.S. workers. But does enhance the fortunes of multinational corporations at home and abroad.

The details of the pact were understandably murky: it was done in secret. But enough details leaked out to demonstrate it was a huge loss for 99 percent of Americans.

Sen. Bernie Sanders of Vermont notes the devastation of U.S. trade agreements.

"Since 2001 we have lost 60,000 factories and five million decent-paying manufacturing jobs," he reports. "We must end our disastrous trade policies. You cannot pass a trade bill like TPP that sends jobs out of our country so that companies here can break unions, force down wages and trim benefits for already wealthy Wall Street executives and investors."

Sanders cited other the miserable trade pacts: North American Free Trade Agreement (NAFTA), Central American Free Trade Agreement (CAFTA) and Permanent Normal Trades Relations (PNTR).

"Fast track turns trade pacts into backdoor means for executive branch officials to set policy on an array of matters under Congress or state legislative authority like patent and copyright laws, immigration policies, food and product safety," he said.

The secrecy power is designed only for revelations that would endanger national security. But Obama put TPP on a "fast track" so the American people could not digest, debate and learn what commentators said about this "fast" scam.

Jim Hightower, a true populist in an age when every politician claims the mantle of populism, is blunt about TPP: "A cabal of global corporations and their friends in the Obama administration waged a wholesale assault on jobs, health, the environment and people's sovereignty."

Moreover, Hightower notes that the trade pact uses "wonkish, gibberistic jargon to mask a corporate boondoggle--the largest trade flimflam in history--negotiated by corporate lobbyists and government lawyers."

The vital interests of the American people render secrecy anathema. Or, as economist Robert Reich put it:

"When corporations, Wall Street and the wealthy get special goodies, the rest of us get shafted. The TPP was being sold as a way to boost the U.S. economy, expand exports and contain China's widening economic influence. In fact, it's just more trickle-down economics."

Other woes of the trade scheme: it gives Big Pharma a virtual patent monopoly. Dean Baker, writing for Truthout, noted: "The Hepatitis-C drug Solvaldi sells for $84,000 a treatment in its patent-protected version in the United States. But a high-quality generic version is available in India for $1,000."

Diane Archer, in an op-edit column for Truthout, says that the hush-hush TPP contains a startling provision: "a Medicare poison pill."

"The bill includes $700 million in Medicare cuts at the end of a 10-year budget period to cover the cost of trade adjustment assistance for displaced workers, Americans who will lose their jobs because of low-cost imports," she writes.

President Obama complained that his Democratic "fellow travelers on progressive issues were 'whupping on' him about trade policy." But as Nation magazine pointed out:

"Obama's dismissal of concerns about TPP undermines his credibility. First, he was unwilling to declassify the text of an agreement that was negotiated behind closed doors with input from corporations who supported it enthusiastically. Second, Obama's suggestion that opponents were just 'making stuff up' denies the experience and insight of progressive critics of free-trade absolutism."

In another Truthout op-ed, Dave Johnson observed that Obama had the chutzpah to pay a laudatory visit to Nike's Oregon headquarters last month. Nike is a super-corporation that grew enormously rich by outsourcing jobs to overseas sweatshops.

"Nike is a company that sets up P.O. box subsidiaries in tax havens to avoid U.S. taxes and a company that uses threats to extort tax breaks from its 'home' state," Johnson writes. "Phil Knight, head of Nike, is now worth $23 billion because America's trade policies encourage companies like Nike to create and move jobs outside the U.S.

"The fact that Knight is the 23rd richest American is one more symbol of the kind of inequality that results from outsourcing fostered by our trade policies. Workers here lose--or never get--jobs. Workers there are paid squat while a few people become vastly wealthy.

"Meanwhile, here's the way the tragic deal works: Massachusetts-based New Balance is already struggling to make its athletic shoes profitable because of cheap imports. TPP removes tariffs from Vietnamese and Malaysian shoes, benefitting Nike and greatly undermining New Balance."

The mainstream media usually dismiss trade accords as arcane stuff of little news value. The truth is otherwise. Unfortunately, Congress passed TPP as it has other trade bills before it.

Sparks Tribune, June 23, 2015

Transgender rights new frontier

Civil rights battles are never won. Nearly 50 years after the great liberator, Martin Luther King, sought freedom for African Americans, racism persists. Equal rights for gays and lesbians are incomplete victories. So is gay marriage.

Now a new struggle has opened for transgender equality. The New York Times tells about it in a long, fact-packed, irrefutable editorial.

"Transgender people are no longer widely regarded as deviants, unfit for dignified workplaces and a disgrace to families," the recent editorial said. "Those who confided in relatives were largely shunned. For most, transitioning on the job was career suicide. Coming out meant going through life as a pariah."

This sad scenario is fortunately changing for 700,000 transgender Americans seeking equality.

Smith, a liberal arts college in Massachusetts, is the latest of prestigious women's colleges to admit transgender women. Students who enroll as women and later come out as men are now welcome at Smith.

President Obama joined the fray after learning that a 17-year-old Ohio transgender girl committed suicide. Religious therapists tried to convert her back to being a boy so she threw herself in front of a tractor-trailer.

"The only way I will rest in peace is if one day transgender people will be treated like human beings," she wrote in suicide note.

Obama responded to this tragedy by urging an end to psychiatric therapies aimed at "repairing" gay, lesbian and transgender youth.

A young male analyst at the CIA, who transitioned on the job in 2013, was worried about losing her career. Not to worry. Colleagues gave her a gift certificate addressed to Ann Taylor. Senior agency officials approved.

The military, however, bans openly transgender people. Obama could end this discrimination with his executive pen power. As so often, he offers soothing words but few good deeds. Many of the closest U.S. allies have integrated transgender people seamlessly into their militaries. One in five transgender people is denied coverage by health care providers.

On a positive note, Medicare lifted its ban on covering gender-change surgery. Another victory came on the employment front. The Justice Department concluded that discrimination on the basis of gender identity, including transgender status, constituted sex discrimination under the Civil Rights Act.

Another positive sign is that prominent transgender people like actress Laverne Cox, Army whistleblower Chelsea Manning and Bruce Jenner, gold-medal Olympian, have come out in recent years.

It's interesting, too, how various individuals cope with being transgender. As the Times said: "Some opt to wear clothes associated with their sex, legally change their names and use new pronouns. Many also undergo hormone replacement therapy and have surgery to transform their bodies. Surgical procedures include chest deduction and augmentation as well as sex-reassignment surgery."

Yet many local jurisdictions throughout the country are still unenlightened, lacking laws protecting transgender people. The fight is far from won.

As for women in general, they are paid on average 78 percent of what men earn per hour. Unfortunately, this is one gender gap unlikely ever to close. Unfortunately, too, a mere 23 women (4.6 percent) are CEOs of Fortune 500 corporations. And: women have directed just 4 percent of top-grossing Hollywood movies in the last dozen years.

Women hardly need reminding that this is still a man's world, a world unlikely ever to change.

P.E.N. and Charlie Hebdo

P.E.N., a literary organization that defends worldwide writers, laudably hands out an annual Freedom of Expression Courage Award. This year the P.E.N. American Center ironically and unlaudably revealed a lack of courage.

Six novelists withdrew from the center's recent award gala in New York and 200 writers signed a letter protesting the 2015 winner, Charlie Hebdo. They complained that the Paris satirical monthly was unworthy of the award because of cartoons critical of Muslims.

Adam Gopnik wrote an essay in The New Yorker defending Charlie Hebdo, declaring that critics had "elided the crucial distinction between blasphemy, which attacks a belief system, and racism, which attacks people."

Gérard Biard, editor of Hebdo who was in New York to receive the award, also defended the publication. "When we mock a religion, we don't knock believers, we don't knock people," Biard insisted. "We mock institutions. We mock ideas."

Hebdo specializes in graphic satires of politicians, public affairs, economics and religions. In the past 10 years it ran 523 covers. Thirty-eight dealt with religions-- Catholic, Jewish, Christian and Muslim. Christianity, with 21, had the most. Just seven dealt with Islam.

The magazine's images may be offensive to believers but the United States and most democracies place a great value on freedom of speech. Above all, it's absurd to kill people because deep religious feelings are hurt. Hebdo carries on a long French tradition of unbridled, viscous satire.

Sparks Tribune, May 19, 2015

Better blustery Trump
than dreary Hillary Clinton

The choice for president of the United States is easy for a Man of the Left: Bernie Sanders.

Sanders won most of the Democratic primaries but his opponent, Hillary Clinton, reaped the majority of delegates to the Democratic Convention in Philadelphia next month. Her big win in the California primary clinched the nomination.

But even before the California vote Clinton had a lock on the superdelegates, those numerous Establishment figures who cling to the past rather than look to the future. And: she has powerful allies on the rules and platform committees to swing things her way.

Sanders, a socialist U.S. senator from Vermont, made a valiant effort but could not wrest the nomination from Clinton, former secretary of state. This is sad because Sanders is a progressive and Clinton a conservative, promising the same-old dreary presidency.

The Sanders election platform called for a modern day revolution, the most progressive since Franklin Roosevelt in the 1930s and 1940s.

Sanders demanded universal health care, a single-payer plan that would cover everyone, including 28 million Americans without any health coverage. It's absurd that the richest country in the world doesn't have national health while smaller and poorer nations do.

Sanders Excoriates Wall Street

"Its six major financial institutions have assets worth 60 percent of our Gross National Product, issue 35 percent of mortgages and two-thirds of credit cards," Sanders declared. "The big corporations earn billions in profits, stash the money in tax havens abroad and pay nothing in income taxes. Billionaire hedge fund managers pay a lower tax rate than teachers or nurses."

Sanders proposed free college education for all who qualify to enter. (Finland, France, Germany, Norway, Sweden and many other nations have free university education.)

The University of California System used to offer free college education but 30 years ago began to charge tuition. Since then college students all over the country have been shackled with debt, taking decades and even lifetimes to pay it off. Sanders would have sought to wipe out that terrible burden.

As is so often the case, the federal government fails to provide things that are essential. College education means more pay and better jobs for individuals and stimulates the national economy. As Michelle Obama chants: "to rise in society go to college."

Sanders urged "bold action on climate control so the planet will be habitable for future generations. The scientific community is nearly unanimous that climate change, caused by human beings, is already damaging Earth.

He lamented the fact that "Congress refuses to appropriate sufficient funds for the nation's infrastructure. Our crumbling roads, bridges, railroads, airports, water systems, wastewater plants, dams and levees are in desperate need of refurbishing."

In short, Sanders made a powerful case to be the next president.

Clinton certainly is qualified to serve in the White House and lead the nation. But she will bring nothing new to the static and stale presidency. Donald Trump will. He is a hugely successful businessman, a real estate tycoon who made a billion dollars in business. Remember, too, Congress can rein in Trump as it does every president.

Be Wary of Gender Politics

Liberal voters this fall should be wary of playing gender politics, of voting for Clinton only because she is a woman. The nation has never had a woman president and now feminists argue that this year provides the chance to make the women's liberation dream come true. The country absolutely needs a woman president--but not Clinton.

A far, far better first woman to become president of the United States is Elisabeth Warren, U.S. senator from Massachusetts. She is a genuine progressive. (I hope she runs for president in 2020 unless the worst happens and Clinton is elected in November, making it difficult for anyone to beat her except Jesus Christ.)

My voting for Trump will astonish those who know my leftish politics. I have never voted for a Republican since I began voting as long ago as 1956. (I voted for the excellent Democratic candidate, Adlai Stevenson, against his Republican rival, the sainted Ike Eisenhower.)

But rather Trump than Clinton. Americans are bloody sick and tired of choosing "the lesser of two evils." That way leads to ever more mediocrity.

Trump, who will be nominated at the GOP convention in Cleveland in July, promises real change. He'll bring excitement to the White House. Clinton promises the politics of yesteryear.

Joe Garofoli, San Francisco Chronicle columnist, observes that Trump "channels the anxieties felt by scores of people who are not billionaires. He soothes their fears by telling them he'll take care of their problems. He comes across as authentic."

Moreover, Garofoli adds, Trump "addresses those fears in bursts of plainspoken, incomplete sentences, the way most people talk."

One California military mother, whose daughter serves in Japan, told an interviewer that she is delighted to hear Trump pledge "to take care of our vets." They deserve it.

The Pentagon today is not taking decent care of veterans.

Republican U.S. House member, Chris Collins, who represents a district in western New York state, makes a powerful case for Trump. Writing a column in the New York Times, Collins says Trump's "lack of political correctness shows that he is independent."

"For too long the political class has denied everyday Americans a real voice in government," Collins declares. "In the election this fall voters are finding a leader who is listening to them over the clamor of Washington's special interests. Voters are speaking loud and clear that they want a leader like Trump. They want a chief executive, not a chief politician."

Endless Tales of Trump

Several positions of Trump are indefensible: proposed restrictions on Muslims entering America, not allowing illegal immigrants from Latin America to stay in this country and elimination of the Affordable Care Act.

Muslims are not the problem, but some Muslims are. Namely, the Taliban. Its followers kill, throw bombs, terrorize civilians, pillage and destroy historic sites. Immigrants take jobs Americans won't: low-paying with long and irregular hours. Obama Care, while not nearly as good as universal health coverage, insures many citizens who wouldn't be covered without it.

Trump University is a fraud, relying on high-pressure sales tactics, employing unqualified instructors and exploiting vulnerable students paying $35,000 to enroll in a real estate class.

Ronald Schnackenberg, sales manager of Trump U., told the New York Times: "Trump University is a fraudulent scheme. It preys on the elderly and uneducated to separate them from their money. He trades on his reputation to sell everything from water and steaks to neckties and education."

USA TODAY reports that the Trumpery has been involved in 3,500 litigations in state and federal courts in the past three decades. "They range from skirmishes with casino patrons to million-dollar real estate suits to personal defamation suits."

No wonder the hot-headed Trump reacts angrily when judges rule against him. Nevertheless, his racist and ethnic slurs are shameful.

Ah, the endless tales of Trump. But some of his proposals are superb.

Violating GOP orthodoxy, Trump would raise taxes on billionaires like himself. He cites the fact that corporations get away with tax murder. He would simplify the tax code, noting that taxpayers spend too much time and money for tax preparers like H&R Block.

He deplores outsourcing. He particularly blasts hedge-fund managers who use the carried-interest loophole to pay a fraction of the taxes they should. He would make Ford and other auto firms "pay a price" for shifting its production abroad.

Trump promises to pull American troops out of South Korea unless Seoul pays more for its bogus "protection." America should yank the troops now with no ifs, ands or buts. Its involvement in the Korean War was wrong from the beginning.

Representative Collins says in defense of Trump: "I see the failures of career politicians in the experiences of hard-working men and women of my district. The safe manufacturer SentrySafe, just closed in Rochester, N.Y., costing hundreds of jobs when the company decamped to Mexico.

"America cannot afford another professional politician residing in the White House. We need a leader who has faced tough, real-life situations before. That leader is Trump.

"One of the many reasons Americans are rallying

behind him is his record of success and commitment to taking the lessons he has learned to the White House. When he talks about being a president who can create jobs, win negotiations and stand up to opponents, people believe him because he has done it before.

"His lack of political correctness shows that he is independent and understands the things people care about."

A close observer of Trump, someone who took the time to read one of his many books, came to admire him saying: "For all the faults of The Boss, he has the techniques of negotiation nailed!"

One thing Sanders, Trump and Clinton agreed on: they all opposed the Trans-Pacific Partnership (TPP). Rightly so.

That and other U.S. trade deals have been a disaster. The 12-country accord does nothing for U.S. workers but enhances the fortunes of multinational corporations at home and abroad.

As Sanders pointed out: "Since 2001 we have lost 60,000 factories and five million decent-paying manufacturing jobs. Congress should not pass a trade bill like TPP that sends jobs out of the country so companies can break unions, force down wages and benefit already wealthy Wall Street executives and investors."

Or, as columnist Jim Hightower, a true populist in an era when every politician claims the mantle of populism, is blunt about TPP: "A cabal of global corporations and their friends in the Obama administration who waged a wholesale assault on jobs, health, the environment and people's sovereignty--a boondoggle, the largest trade flimflam in history."

No presidential candidate in history has hauled so much political baggage as Donald Trump. Yet Clinton, too, carries a great deal of baggage.

Clinton Triumph Bodes Ill

Clinton has served the wealthy and powerful like lawyers and technicians. Raise wages? Yes, she would, but never says how much. She is beholden to corporate power. After all, she served on the corporate board of Walmart.

Women at Walmart are paid less than men. They advance to management positions at lower rates than men even though their performance reviews are higher. Clinton made no effort to combat this sexism when she was on the Walmart board. Neither did she object that Walmart is violently anti-union while women make up the majority of workers. This is a woman's inequality issue that demands an outraged cry.

Clinton rakes in $200,000 for many speaking engagements. She earned $11 million in 2014 for 51 speeches to banks and industries. She took in $675,000 for speeches for Goldman-Sachs.

The New York Times editorialized: " 'Everybody does it' is her mischievous-child defense for making closed-door, richly paid speeches for big banks but refusing to release transcripts. At candidate forums she gives a terrible answer: she'll release transcripts 'if everybody does it and that includes Republicans.'

"By stonewalling on transcripts Clinton suggests that she is not trustworthy and makes her own rules. Most important, she damages her credibility among Democrats who beg her to show them she'd run an accountable and transparent White House."

Clinton is called a liberal but she is a centrist as nearly all presidents are, including the incumbent President Obama. She is a middle-of-the-roader like her husband, former President Bill Clinton.

Clinton's Hawkish Record

Clinton is an unabashed hawk. She supported the

invasion of Iraq, the long occupation and counter-insurgency in that country.

As secretary of state she backed escalation of the Afghanistan War, pressed President Obama to arm Syrian rebels and endorsed airstrikes against the ruling Syrian regime. She supported intervention in Libya with drone strikes.

As Democratic U.S senator from New York for eight years her record was doubly hawkish. She was the only Democratic senator who made false claims that Saddam Hussein gave sanctuary to Al-Qaeda.

Clinton has a dark legacy in the Mexican drug war, according to Jesse Franzblau in a foreign policy analysis for Truthout: "U.S. law prohibits aid to nations guilty of human rights violations. Yet Clinton's state department regularly ignored widespread drug-linked corruption and torture in Mexico."

Clinton opposes single-payer health care that Canada and most European nations are blessed with.

Writer Carl Bernstein noted that Clinton waged a lengthy battle to discredit Gennifer Flowers, an actress who had a long affair with Bill Clinton. Hillary "dished" her as "trailer trash." Lisa Featherstone wrote in a Truthout op-ed piece: "Clinton's feminism is shallow. It is concerned with women at the top of society while condoning abuse of those without power. It's elitism."

As president, Bill Clinton pushed his punitive crime bill of 1994. His First Lady supported it with an ugly remark: "Young criminals are not just gangs of kids anymore. They are super-predators."

In 1996 President Clinton's penal budget was twice the amount allocated to food stamps. He wanted "to end welfare as we know it." He railed against "welfare queens" and "big government." Mere nods of agreement from the First Lady.

As Governor of Arkansas for 11 years Clinton was

most vulnerable on tax inequity. He raised taxes in a poor state regressively, hurting low-income people. He was weak on social issues and the environment.

But there are many other indictments of would-be president Clinton. Namely: emails. While serving as secretary of state she used her family's private email server for official emails rather than use proper State Department channels.

She destroyed 32,000 of those emails she deemed private, a clear violation of State Department rules and federal laws governing official recordkeeping. She destroyed them with the incredible declaration that the emails were personal and not work-related.

The State Department's independent watchdog, the Office of the Inspector General, issued a devastating report on Clinton's email management: "practically everything Clinton has said about her use of a private server is false."

Still another Clinton gambit while secretary of state that should bar her from being president: she made weapons transfers to the Saudis a top priority while the Clinton Foundation accepted millions of dollars in donations from the Kingdom of Saudi Arabia and the weapons manufacturer Boeing.

"Despite the brutal attacks on Yemen and egregious domestic human rights violations, Saudi Arabia remains the number one U.S. ally in the Arab world," Benjamin Medea wrote in an op-ed for PINKtan.

"It's hard to exaggerate the enormity and hi-tech nature of Saudi weapons purchases from the United States. The decade from 2000 to 2010 constitutes the most enormous military sale in history. Weapons valued at 100 billion dollars included F-15 bombers, Apache and Blackhawk helicopters, missile defense systems, bombs and armored vehicles."

To sum up, the Clintons will use political influence,

money and connections to extend their dynasty for another tenure in the White House: Bill Clinton, the man from Hope, Ark., and Hillary Clinton who hopes to become the first woman president. Her record makes plain she does not deserve it.

Reno News & Review, June 30, 2016

Rich justices bare bias

The Supreme Court under Chief Justice Roberts has long shown its conservative biases. Its latest: fierce anti-unionism.

Law professors often write articles about the shortcomings of the federal judicial system but never get to the root of the problem. Namely, Supreme Court justices are lawyers.

Lawyers are legalistic, not humanistic. They are narrow-minded. They "follow the law" of yesterday, not the views of modern society. They favor corporations rather than consumers. They tend to be conservative. You don't get ahead in the legal business by being liberal.

Most federal judges are rich. In two terms President Reagan appointed 279 judges. The majority had a net worth of $400,000. One fifth were millionaires. Wealthy judges are unlikely to rule for the working class.

And so it was in the recent Supreme Court ruling, Friedrichs v. California Teachers Association: a blatant slap at public-sector unions (teachers, police and firefighters).

Here's how Nation magazine described it: "Friedrichs was thrown together by business-backed, anti-union advocacy groups. The district court and appeals court approved the suit without hearing all evidence nor much oral argument."

The Supreme Court's conservative majority found an excuse: the First Amendment. The amendment forbids forcing public workers to support a union they decline to join, that they cannot be compelled to pay for advocacy they disagree with.

The argument is lame. The non-union workers are getting a free ride, union benefits that they have not paid for. The benefits of paying union dues are enormous: collective bargaining and lobbying for higher pay, shorter hours and better working conditions.

Roberts called such (the free benefits) "really insignificant" and "not posing much of a problem." That's easy for a wealthy man to say, a man who got rich by serving as a corporate lawyer.

A proper decision would have been to overturn the lower courts in the interest of fairness and justice. But as the Roberts Court so often does, it manufactures raw political decisions rather than making high-minded judicial rulings.

Nibble, Nibble, Nibble

The Supreme Court keeps nibbling around the death penalty but refuses to abolish it. It simply quarrels over the minor details and ways of execution.

In a recent decision, Hurst v. Florida, the court ruled that Florida did not give jurors a sufficient role in deciding whether defendants should be put to death.

Justice Sonia Sotomayor wrote for the court: "The Sixth Amendment requires a jury, not a judge, to uphold a death sentence.

Nor is it enough to "nibble, nibble little mouse," as Grimm's "Hansel and Gretel" phrases it. The evil of capital punishment should end in this sometimes uncivilized America.

Terribly Prudish Religion

When Iranian President Hassan Rouhani paid a state visit to Italy recently his host, Italian Prime Minister Renzi, prudishly ordered classic nude statutes covered with boxes.

Iran's state religion is Sharia law (strict Muslim), a religion so backward it insists that great art be shielded. Renzi wanted to avoid embarrassing his host but succeeded in embarrassing the Italian people.

Next Rouhani went to France on a state visit. There, French Prime Minister Hollande would have no such squeamishness: he canceled lunch because Rouhani insisted on a halal menu, which prohibits alcohol.

To paraphrase a wonderful French expression, the

wine-drinking French call lunch without wine a day without sunshine.

Chess and Satan

More religious nonsense. Saudi Arabia's top cleric has declared in a fatwa that chess is forbidden, "the work of Satan."

A fatwa against chess? Inconceivable yet it is hardly astonishing in the "holiest" religious nation in the world.

The Grand Mufti, Sheikh Abdulaziz Al-Sheikh, overlooks the fact that chess has been enormously popular in the Muslim world for centuries. Indeed, the head of the Saudi chess association defiantly held a chess tournament in Mecca despite the fatwa.

Such an austere interpretation of Islam forbids socializing between men and women who are not related. It bans most music. It is an inhuman view by an arch-reactionary nation.

More Religious Madness

The latest Saudi religious madness: convicting a stateless Palestinian poet of apostasy, sentencing him to eight years in prison, imposing physical punishment of 800 lashes and demanding repentance.

His crime? Publishing poetry that offends prudes.

Sparks Tribune, Feb. 9, 2016

Audubon and dying courtesy

Ralph Waldo Emerson, intellectual guru of mid-19th century America, received a copy of "Leaves of Grass" by the then unknown author, Walt Whitman.

Emerson was a busy man writing essays, reviews and poems while facing a constant stream of visitors.

One two-time visitor was Oscar Wilde, Irish playwright, novelist and poet. After the first visit Wilde, who was lecturing in America, wrote to Emerson: "Before I leave America I must see you again. There is no one in this great world of America who I honor and love so much."

Yet Emerson, as busy as he was, took the time to write Whitman a five-page letter. It included: "I greet you at the beginning of a great career." He was as right as he was perceptive. Whitman became what many have called America's greatest poet.

Emerson's courtesy is often unobserved today by people far less busy. I wrote two books recently, self-published like the first edition of "Leaves of Grass." Many recipients did not have the courtesy to reply. In the vernacular: no class.

Today emails make acknowledgement a matter of four words and 10 seconds: "Got your book. Thanks."

I sent two books to the journalism dean at the University of Nevada, Reno. No reply. I sent books to several journalism professors. No reply. I sent a book dedicated to a Reno editor. No reply. I sent a book to a UNR political science professor. No reply.

I filled the office box of a UNR journalism professor, who teaches the First Amendment class. The items included a DVD lecture series on the history of the Supreme Court, my book on the Roberts Court and several articles about the court. No reply.

Impolite people remind you of the line in Sartre's "No Exit": "Hell is other people."

However, one recipient of my books is a class guy: Dennis Myers, news editor of the Reno News & Review. He not only replies, he offers insights and poses questions.

Which brings me to the work at hand, a bad book about Whitman. It is "In Walt We Trust" by John Marsh, a Penn State English professor. The subtitle is absurd: "How a Queer Socialist Poet Can Save America from Itself."

Whitman was not a socialist and America cannot be "saved" by his poetry. His poems cannot show us how to live and how to die, as the book jacket absurdly insists.

Marsh's book is poorly written, full of irrelevancies and ridiculous references to himself. It needs a stern editor. This is hardly surprising. Marsh is a PhD who uses academic words like "existential" and "canonical." He writes such nonsense as: "Every life is irrelevant" and "Whitman saved my life."

Marsh rambles on about Camden, N.J., where Whitman lived his last years. Marsh suffers from the historian's vice: Whitman "would seem," "appears to have meant" and "may or may not have." His book uses lame qualifiers like "rather" and "somewhat" and unnecessary words like "of course." Thoreau visited Whitman but left mystified. Why? Marsh doesn't say.

He wastes a page on Tertullian, third century Christian theologian. He has ridiculous digressions like: "if we want Whitman to like us, and frankly, that is all I want these days." He asks if Whitman was gay. It doesn't matter. His poetry is what matters.

Marsh writes that he "dislikes" Whitman's tomb in Camden. His adulation prevents him from denouncing an enormously expensive, grandiose monument designed by Whitman. The tomb belies the words of "Song of Myself": "I bequeath myself to the dirt to grow from the grass I love, / If you want me again look for me under your boot soles."

The flyleaf boasts: "The book is a mix of biography, literary criticism, manifesto and a kind of self-help you're unlikely to encounter anywhere else." Let's hope not. Better to read the first of the many edited and rewritten editions of "Leaves of Grass" and judge for yourself.

My favorite quotes from "Leaves":
- "Walt Whitman, of Manhattan the son, / Turbulent, fleshy, sensual, eating, drinking and breeding."
- "Animals do not sweat and whine about their condition, / They do not lie awake in the dark and weep for their sins, / They do not make me sick discussing their duty to God."
- "I hail the joys of dear companions with their merry words and laughing faces / I cherish the plenteous dinner and strong carouse."
- "I hear the annual singing of the children in St. Paul's cathedral in London, / With the symphonies and oratorios of Beethoven, Handel or Haydn."
- "Away with themes of war! Away with war itself!"
- "I have loved the earth, sun, animals. I have despised riches / Devoted my income and labor to others and hated tyrants."
- "The great Idea, O my brethren, is the mission of poets."

Sparks Tribune, June 2, 2015

Religious extremists delay flights

The First Amendment guarantees "the free exercise" of religion but that hardly means people can exercise that freedom on airlines.

More and more ultra-orthodox Jews and Muslims are violating the travel space of people who just want to fly peacefully to their destinations, the New York Times reports.

A woman was assigned an aisle seat on a flight from New York to London but a man refused to sit next to her. He declared that his religion prohibited him from sitting by a woman not his wife. Irritated, but eager to get underway, she moved.

Another woman was sitting in a middle seat and her husband on the aisle. A man asked her to switch positions for religious reasons. She refused. To her it was intrusive and sexist.

The two cases illustrate the growing number of seating conflicts caused especially by ultra-orthodox Jews on flights to Israel. The demonstrators cause disruption and departure delays.

One flight arrived an hour late because a Haredi (ultra-Orthodox) balked at sitting between two women, calling it a matter of faith.

A wag recommended a full-body suit, entirely kosher, to "protect" the ultra-orthodox. But the problem is no joke. More passengers are declining to move.

One woman refused to switch seats because her husband finds flying less stressful if seated on the aisle.

A blogger declared: "There is a vast difference between the freedom to exercise religion and religious interference. Refusal to take a seat and delaying a flight is crossing that boundary.

"As for Haredi men, they are unruly and asinine and a threat to public order."

The demonstrators are not just annoying. They are stealing other people's time.

Russian artists battle censors

One of America's greatest plays is "Who's Afraid of Virginia Woolf," written by Edward Albee in 1961. The dialogue is cutting, sniping and nasty. A married couple comes home at 2 a.m. from a party. Martha opens with a roar: "Jesus..." George: "Shhhhhh." Martha still roaring: "...H. Christ."

That curse word would not be permitted in Russia today. A law passed by a puritanical Duma (parliament) last year prohibited obscenities in public performances.

The law is reminiscent of the 1930s when the Nazi regime in Germany denounced "degenerate art." Obviously the Dumaites have not read history.

Also banned in Russia: a Siberian production of Wagner's "Tannhäuser" because a backdrop showed an image of Christ in the crotch of a naked woman. Worse: Moscow's Pussy Riot punk rock group was tossed in jail for two years for insulting the dictator, President Vladimir Putin.

Putin normally tells the Duma what to do but the uproar over the ban on obscenities forced him to back off. He told an angry group of writers that Tolstoy and Chekhov didn't need cursing. But, he said, "You, the writers, know best."

Tolstoy and Chekhov, Russian literary lions, were writing in the 19th century when obscenities in literature were uncommon. Today, let writers write.

Footnote: the banned-in-Boston censors erased Albee's opening curse word, insisting on a euphemism instead. Albee outfoxed them. His substitute passed muster: "Mary H. Magdalene."

Journalism chairman dies

Bob Kaiser, chairman of the journalist department at

the University of Nevada, Reno, from 1981 to 1984, died recently at the age of 84.

After ordination into the Jesuit order, he covered Vatican II for Time magazine. That's doubtless why he cared more about Catholicism than running the journalism department.

But I'll never knock him. He lured me to the godforsaken desert of Nevada where I taught for 32 years. While teaching in Reno I met and married my beloved wife.

When I came to Reno for a job interview, Bob and I hit it off immediately. He impressed me by his professional reporting background in a field increasingly dominated by the dreaded PhDs. He couldn't abide the nonsense of social science "journalism" and the academic jargon of double-domes ill suited to teach reporting, editing and writing.

Bob met me at the airport and booked me in the Ramada Inn. We talked happily at a bar for a couple hours.

Looking around the inn's casino, I was amazed at the densely packed slot machines and gambling tables in every nook and cranny. I couldn't believe one woman who was feeding five slot machines simultaneously--and brooked no intruder who tried to grab one of "her" machines.

One morning I looked out my Ramada room window and was amazed again to see the snow-capped peaks of Mt. Rose and Slide Mountain, towering over Reno and gleaming in early sunlight.

Seventy-eight people had applied for the teaching job. I was one of the three brought to the campus by the search committee. Fortunately, I was chosen. After 15 years of newspapering and 13 years of teaching at a university "back East," I found a happy home "out West."

Sparks Tribune, April 28, 2015

People and Places

Papal 'rock star' keeps moldy doctrine

Two hundred and 70 bishops from 120 countries issued a disheartening report after a recent three-week Vatican synod discussing family matters for the world's 1.2 billion Catholics.

Marianne Duddy-Burke, executive director of DignityUSA, called the document "deeply disappointing," one that blocked "civil and moral equality for our community." That community: an organization of gay, lesbian, bisexual and transgender Catholics.

A Vatican official, fired recently after admitting publicly that he was gay and in a relationship, sent an angry letter to Pope Francis. The official, the Rev. Krzysztof Charamsa, wrote that he was making the lives of gay and transgender people a hell. He added that the church is persecuting gay Catholics, causing them and their families immeasurable suffering.

Many conservative bishops at the synod called those who remarry without getting an annulment, adulterers living in sin. They said the church cannot change its doctrine that marriage is indissoluble. But some bishops called that "insensitive, even cruel, because it refuses to take personal circumstances into account."

No wonder the New York Times called it "the most contentious and momentous meeting of bishops in the 50 years since Vatican II."

The synod exposed deep fault lines between traditionalists wanting to shore up doctrines and those who want the church to be more open to Catholics who are divorced, gay and single parents.

Pope Francis, papal rock star, has won worldwide praise for being a nice guy. But that is hardly praiseworthy. The sad truth is that the pope has changed none of the musty doctrines of the Roman Catholic Church.

Francis made a temporary absolution for Catholics "who bear in their heart the scar" of abortion and repent during the upcoming Jubilee or Holy Year.

But Katie Klabusich in a Truthout news analysis countered that 95 percent of Catholics have neither struggled over nor regretted their abortions. It is not the "existential or moral ordeal" characterized by the pope.

"I grew up Catholic and attended a Jesuit university," Erin Matson, co-director of the reproductive justice organization, ReproAction, said.

"The official teachings of the Catholic Church on sexuality, including but not limited to abortion, harm people around the world," he pointed out. "The views of the Vatican are deeply out of step with the views of Catholics.

"Women who have had abortions have done nothing wrong. They have nothing to apologize for. Pope Francis is not changing any doctrine on abortion."

The Rev. Harry Knox, president of the Religious Coalition for Reproductive Choice, is blunt: Francis starts off with compassion "but quickly turns to more shame for women."

"Women have abortions for many reasons," he noted. "What a woman really needs from her clergy is someone ready and able to have deep pastoral conversations about the decision."

One in three Catholic women have had one or more abortions. Catholic women oppose criminalizing abortion by a margin of 2-1. This is the reality of Catholic women's lives, not some obsolete papal decree.

The church is adamantly against birth control yet most Catholics use it, forced to be grossly hypocritical about their faith. Moreover, Garry Wills, Catholic writer, ridicules the idea that using a contraceptive is "a mortal sin for which Catholics would go to hell if they died unrepentant."

Still more reactionaryism: the church is woefully short

of priests but will not allow women into the priesthood. It deems women unequal to men. Sister Louise Akers, head of the Sisters of Charity, rightly calls the Catholic Church "the last bastion of sexism."

And still more backwardness: the church insists that priests be celibate. Celibacy is unnatural. Probably most priestly pedophilia can be attributed to celibacy. The church doesn't allow divorced Catholics to take communion. It should. Communion is central to Catholicism.

And still more backward doctrines: the church prohibits the use of condoms even to prevent AIDS--a clear example of head-in-the-sand dogma. The church opposes premarital sex, a view contrary to human nature, and therefore practiced by most Catholics.

And still more dithering: the streamlined annulment procedure recently unveiled by the pope supposedly simplifies the arduous gauntlet of red tape. A worthwhile outcome is dubious.

Annulment proceedings can take a year or more and cost upwards of $1,000 in "bribes" to annulling bishops. Francis asks that annulments be granted free. Asking is not promulgating.

The church needs genuine reform, not cosmetics and pretty talk.

Pope Francis recently canonized Junipero Serra, founder of Spanish missions in California. He called Serra "a friend of humanity." Keener judgment would call him unworthy of sainthood.

The mission's main purpose was to convert the "heathen" Indians to Catholicism. Indigenous Americans rightly denounce Serra for trying to destroy their culture.

His missionaries sought to convert Indians to Christianity. Serra required Indians to learn Spanish. He advocated using whips to lash those who spoke the native language and followed native culture. Indians were forced to labor under brutal and sometimes fatal conditions.

Sainthood should not be bestowed on someone who forces conversion at the end of a whip.

Panel praises pope

Pope Francis in his homilies, press conferences, interviews and offhand remarks to visitors has impressed observers worldwide by his humility, friendliness and earthiness.

Typical comments by all-faiths panelists published recently in the Reno Gazette-Journal: "A witness to the world"..."A visible role model"..."An inspiration"... "Fountain of grace"... "Uplifts the very soul"... "Lover of all mankind"..."A Christ-like pope."

Such extensive praise disturbs Harvey Cox, a Harvard divinity professor. He fears a "cult of personality," making the pope less effective.

Kenneth Lucey, philosophy and religion professor at the University of Nevada, Reno, was the only RGJ panelist who dissented from the adulation. He rightly urged the ordination of women. But Lucey should have gone farther, urging Francis to abolish the dogmas against abortion, birth control, homosexuality, gay marriage, divorce, transgenders and married priests.

Oh, the pope utters fine biblical lines like "judge not that ye be not judged." But he refuses to go to the root of the problem for most worldwide Catholics.

Until he approves those essential changes, Francis remains mired in the past. All the encomiums heaped on him by leaders of all religious faiths will not hide the bleaker truths.

The headline over comments by the faith panelists proclaimed: "Can Pope Francis change the world?" That is a terrible cliché as well as being terribly untrue. Lucey conceded in his panel segment that the pope "could change the world by altering the rules of the church." But making

Catholic women priests will hardly "change the world." Nor will married Catholic priests.

As for the pope's marvelous appeal for social justice and rightful denunciation of the "tyranny of capitalism," its "trickle-down theory," its "free market" and his rightful urging of climate control, those are matters that he can do nothing about.

Conservative editors of Time proclaimed Francis "person of the year" for 2013. Citations by magazine editors: "The People's Pope...He prays constantly, even when while waiting for the dentist...He has retired the papal Mercedes for a scuffed-up Ford Focus...No red shoes, no gilded cross...General aura of merriment not usually associated with princes of the church."

The men and women of the year should do greater things than just being popular.

Sainthood and bad popes

The Catholic Church and the saint business can be unholy. Bad popes are often canonized for no other reason than that they have been pontiffs. Such is the case of the recent bestowal of sainthood on a bad pope: John Paul II.

Maureen Dowd, columnist for the New York Times, is a Catholic yet critical of the Vatican and popes like John Paul. She wrote a recent column bluntly headlined: "A saint he ain't." She tells why:

• John Paul presided over the Catholic Church during nearly three decades of the gruesome pedophilia scandal.

• He shamed the papacy by "giving sanctuary to Cardinal Law, a horrendous enabler of child abuse, who resigned in disgrace as archbishop of Boston."

• He issued a defense of the dastardly Mexican priest, Marcial Maciel Degollado, a pedophile, womanizer, embezzler and drug addict. He ran his order, the Legionaries of Christ, like an ATM and a cult for himself and the Vatican for 65 years." He was probably the worst sexual predator in Catholic history.

• The church is giving its biggest honor to the man "who could have fixed the spreading stain and did nothing. It is wounding and ugly when the church signals to those thousands of betrayed and damaged victims that they are a mere fading asterisk."

But, alas, Ms. Dowd tells only half of John Paul's misdeeds. Michael Gallagher, Truthout columnist, tells the other half. He writes:

• "John Paul, in his eagerness to gain America's material support in liberating his native Poland, had no qualms about selling Latin America down the river."

• He condemned Liberation Theology, acclaimed by Latin American bishops, for its key tenet: "the preferential option for the poor." Latin American Catholics, using the teachings of Jesus, wanted to liberate the poor from unjust economic, political and social conditions. It was nothing less than "an interpretation of Christian faith through the poor's suffering and struggle." Nevertheless, John Paul dismissed Liberation Theology as Marxist-inspired. (There is more Marx in Jesus than Christians admit.)

• John Paul made one of his favorites, the pedophile monk, Hans Groër, archbishop of Vienna.

• After John Paul's long-delayed response to pedophilia, he wallowed in self-pity "that this should fall upon me in my old age."

• He refused to attend the funeral of the martyred Archbishop Romero in 1980, "giving the green light to the murderous Salvadoran junta eager to get rid of pious meddlers." The situation has echoes of the murder in Canterbury Cathedral of Archbishop Becket in 1170 by four knights in the entourage of King Henry II. The king is said to have asked: "Will no one rid me of this turbulent priest?" The knights did.

• The Salvadoran junta in 1980 sent a death squad

to rape and kill two Maryknoll nuns and an American missionary in El Salvador.

• In 1981 the junta dispatched an elite military unit, trained at Ft. Benning, Georgia, to murder six Jesuits on the faculty of the Central American University at San Salvador, El Salvador.

• The papal nuncio to the United States, Archbishop Pio Laghi, with John Paul's approval, "functioned as President Reagan's go-between with the Contra terrorists in Nicaragua whose favorite victims were doctors, nurses, literacy workers and campesino coffee workers."

After devastating a bad pope and horrible saint, columnist Dowd extols a good pope worthy of sainthood: John XXIII.

The saintly John XXIII convened the historic Vatican II, aggiornamento, "a bringing up to date," an open window on the Catholic Church. He embraced Jews and opened a conversation on birth control.

John XXIII, the good, was made a saint the same day as John Paul, the bad. It was one more example of cynical Vatican machinations, a subterfuge unworthy of Pope Francis.

Opulence is out

The simplicity of Pope Francis has been an object lesson to all Catholics: he lives in modest Vatican quarters. Yet the Archbishop of Atlanta, Wilton Gregory, planned to build a luxurious $2.2 million mansion until a backlash of his parishioners made him drop the plan.

Archbishop Gregory lamely rationalized that "the world has changed." Perhaps he never heard of the modest living style of his pope. But surely he has read the Gospels. Matthew 6:24 reads: "Ye cannot serve God and mammon."

'Saint' Dorothy Day

Pope Francis declared before Congress on Sept. 26: "In these times when social concerns are so important, I cannot fail to mention the Servant of God, Dorothy Day, who founded the Catholic Worker Movement."

Unfortunately, he did not say that Day deserves to be a Catholic saint.

He did not mention that she also co-founded the Catholic Worker with Peter Maurin in 1933, the best "unknown" newspaper in America. It is still published today.

The eight-page monthly is packed with progressive articles that match the leading leftist magazines in the country, The Nation and The Progressive. What's particularly amazing is that The Worker carries the banner of the conservative Catholic Church.

Day is far more worthy of being a saint than the many nonentities who have been canonized. Some people object that she was a heretic and an unmarried mother who had an abortion. None of those objections matter.

Her record for sainthood is clear:

• She wrote a biography of her favorite saint, Thérèse of Lisieux, the Little Flower. Day called her 'the people's saint.' "

• In her autobiography, "The Long Loneliness," published in 1952, she spoke of her concern for the unfortunate, her fight for women's suffrage, socialism, the Industrial Workers of the World and becoming a Catholic.

• Day was a Christian through and through. In the Worker for November of 1936 she wrote: "Christ did not need pomp and circumstance to prove Himself the Son of God"…"If Our Lord were alive today, he would say, as He said to St. Peter, 'Put up thy sword' "…"Prince of Peace, Christ our King, Christ our brother and Christ the Son of Man."

Day started and led a lay movement that operated without authorization of the Catholic Church. The Worker took and still takes positions far ahead of the Vatican, most newspapers and television. She prophetically anticipated themes of Vatican II: ecumenism, liturgical renewal, religious freedom, the right of conscience and opposition to racism and anti-Semitism.

She denounced war. She was jailed for protesting Civil Defense drills. She called preparation for nuclear war blasphemy.

As a teenager she was an avid reader of such writers as Upton Sinclair, Jack London, Darwin, Aldous Huxley, Kropotkin, Dostoevsky, Tolstoy and Gorky. So it is no surprise that in the Worker of May 1951, Day wrote that Marx, Lenin and Mao Tse-tung were animated by brotherhood.

In 1917 she was arrested for picketing the White House on behalf of women's suffrage. She backed the suffragette Silent Sentinels organized by Alice Paul. The cost: 15 days in jail, 10 of them on a hunger strike.

As a journalist in 1933, Day covered the Hunger March of the Unemployed Councils for Commonweal magazine and the Farmers' Conference for America magazine in Washington, D.C.

Above all, she fought for the poor, for justice and for humanity. Dorothy Day clearly should be made a saint.

Reno News & Review, Nov. 12, 2015

Ali: profile in courage outside boxing ring

"I ain't got nothing against them Vietcong."

Muhammad Ali

Muhammad Ali, the charismatic and controversial boxing titan, was given a fine farewell in an obituary tribute by Robert Lipsyte in the New York Times.

"Ali was the most thrilling, if not the best heavyweight ever, carrying into the ring a physically lyrical, unorthodox boxing style that fused speed, agility and power more seamlessly than any fighter before him," Lipsyte wrote.

"An agile mind, a buoyant personality, a brash self-confidence with his fists, using a patter of inventive doggerel. He converted from Christianity to Islam, changing his 'slave name' of Cassius Clay to one bestowed by the separatist Islamic group, the Nation of Islam ('Black Muslims')."

Ali, who died recently at 74 of Parkinson's disease, was three times heavyweight champion. But to me the most significant thing about him was his opposition to the Vietnam War and refusal to be drafted into the Army.

He was originally disqualified by the Louisville, Ky., selective service board because of his substandard score on a mental aptitude test. But he was reclassified 1A in February 1966 after a lower standard was established. He was now eligible to go to war.

But he balked at the mere thought of fighting in a war, telling a mostly hostile press that he had nothing against the Vietcong. To my intense sorrow, my all-time favorite sports writer, Red Smith of the New York Herald Tribune, wrote this ugly paragraph:

"Squealing over the possibility that the military might call him up, Cassius makes himself as sorry a spectacle as those unwashed punks who picket and demonstrate against the war."

On the positive side of the press, however, broadcaster Howard Cosell defended Ali's decisions. Cosell was responsible for keeping Ali on television during his forced interval from the ring, both as an interview subject and commentator during boxing matches.

In April 1967 Ali refused to be drafted and requested conscientious objection status. A lower federal court denied his right to both stances. He was stripped of his heavyweight title by the boxing commission. Ali did not box again for three and one-half years, losing precious years of his athletic prime.

The Supreme Court, after appeals crawled through the legal process, ruled on June 26, 1971. It unanimously reversed the lower court.

The court of public opinion also finally came to Ali's side, agreeing that the Vietnam War was one of the many unjust U.S. wars.

As for Ali the boxer, Jim Murray of the Los Angeles Times wrote: "He no longer had fights. He gave recitals."

Give poet Elizabeth Alexander the last word. It's called "Narrative: Ali," subtitled "a poem in twelve rounds." Just a few lines from round 12:

"They called me 'the fistic pariah.'

"They said I didn't love my country,

"Called me a race-hater...waited for me

"to come out on a stretcher, shot at me,

"hexed me, cursed me...."

The truth is Ali loved his country as anyone does who has the courage to shout out its wrongs.

Okinawans Outraged by Slayings

The U.S. military has stopped partying on seedy Gate Street with its strip of bars and clubs because a 20-year-old Okinawan woman was recently murdered on the southern Japanese island. The woman's decomposing body was found in a suitcase near the huge Air Force base.

Okinawans were outraged by the murder but it was hardly the first time they were angered by crimes, violence and noise from American personnel stationed at the Air Force base and the U.S Marine Corps Air Station.

An American military contractor, who is a Marine veteran, has been arrested in the killing.

Why the U.S. still has military bases in Okinawa 71 years after the end of World War II can only be explained by the sickening endless and boundless worldwide U.S. imperialism. Okinawa is still a U.S. colony.

Blame President Obama, the so-called man of peace, for a totally unjust display of military might in Okinawa.

Vatican Leaks and Staged Trial

The Vatican City constantly seethes with conspiracy, intrigue and mystery, always surprising for a supposedly holy place.

The latest to breech the wall of secrecy is a Vatican consultant, Francesca Chaouqui. She is accused of stealing and leaking confidential documents to two journalists who wrote tell-all books about Vatican mismanagement and corruption.

She is a scapegoat given a show trial by Vatican prosecutors in "Vatileaks 2" before being sent to jail for 15 years. Again the Vatican is trying to muzzle free speech and squelch embarrassing criticisms.

Vatican officials--incredibly--are calling the disclosures "a threat to its securty." What it really is: a threat to frequent embarrassments.

Sparks Tribune, June 14, 2016

Political genius source
of the musical Hamilton

Alexander Hamilton
By Ron Chernow
731 pages, The Penguin Press, 2004

The sold-out smash hit "Hamilton," the hip-hop musical now on Broadway, is reaping astounding plaudits.

It has been nominated for 16 Tony Awards, more than any other show in Broadway history. The nominators deemed the show worthy in every category of theater-making: acting, writing, directing, dance, music and design. Seven "Hamilton" performers were cited for Tonys.

The super-show is based on Ron Chernow's history of Alexander Hamilton, the nation's first Secretary of the Treasury.

Whatever the hip-hop version, Chernow tells the remarkable story of an unsung American hero. Hamilton was principal designer of the federal government. He was the most important of the Founders who never became president.

Hamilton, a brave battlefield hero, was a youthful aide-de-camp to General Washington. (Washington called him "my boy.")

Hamilton railed at the lack of sufficient money from Congress to support the independence struggle. He was a member of the Constitutional Convention and leading author of the historic "The Federalist Papers."

He headed the Federalist Party, forerunner of today's Republican Party. He established the nation's tax and budget systems and the central bank. He was an unabashed apologist for business and the profit motive. No wonder he has been called the patron saint of Wall Street.

In the Federalist essays he pushed the idea that federal judges should serve for life, subject to impeachment only for misconduct, not for unpopular decisions. The absolute independence of the federal judiciary is essential, he argued.

In Federalist essay 78 he wrote: "no legislative act contrary to the Constitution can be valid."

Supreme Court Chief John Marshall embedded that Hamiltonian view in the Constitution. Marshall gave the nation the doctrine of judicial review in the Marbury v. Madison decision of 1803, declaring "an act of the legislature repugnant to the Constitution is void."

The Federalist essays reveal "the extraordinary breadth of his thinking," Chernow writes.

That is fact. But Chernow, like many historians, is often plagued by conjectureitis: "Hamilton might have," "he must have," "he could have" or "probably." If historians don't know the facts they should admit it.

Chernow guesses that Hamilton became an insatiable reader of the classics. He writes that he probably read works by Plutarch, Machiavelli and the poetry of Alexander Pope. He thinks Hamilton was born on Nevis, British West Indies, in the Caribbean. But mostly the book is packed with facts.

Among this copious reading was the art of warfare and military discipline. Although a British subject, Hamilton proved invaluable to young America. His father vanished, his mother and all relatives died by the time he was 14, leaving him an orphan.

But the impoverished lad was soon arguing for and fighting for colonial independence. He attended King's College in New York (now Columbia) and graduated from the College of New Jersey (now Princeton). At the battle of Yorktown his valiant performance was death-defying.

He was a fierce proponent of abolition 75 years before the Civil War. He demanded black battalions for the war effort. (As British essayist Samuel Johnson complained:

"Why do we hear the loudest yelps for liberty from slave drivers?")

Hamilton rightly complained that the Articles of Confederation promised little more than a fragile alliance of 13 miniature republics. He denounced the masses. He called democracy folly because the politicians simply catered to the popular will.

As a lawyer, he defended colonial Tories who criticized the revolution. "He was not a politician seeking popularity but a statesman determined to change minds," Chernow writes.

This was the man Aaron Burr murdered in a duel in 1804 in Weehawken, N.J. The two had a long-standing bitterness and antagonism. After Hamilton savagely attacked Burr in a pamphlet, he demanded the fatal duel.

The book is repetitious, 300 pages too long and tells non-scholars more than they want to know about Hamilton. Chernow, however, does give us a much greater appreciation of Hamilton. Indeed, he suggests that Hamilton was the greatest of the Founders.

Be that as it may, Hamilton deserves the accolade of British statesman Lord Bryce: "the one founding father who has not received his due from posterity."

Sparks Tribune, June 7, 2016

Irish now target abortion ban

Young liberals are lifting the Irish from the shackles of Catholicism.

Ireland, the most Catholic country on the globe, recently passed by a whopping 62 percent a constitutional amendment allowing same-sex marriage.

The vote was amazing. Eighty-five percent of the Irish population is Catholic. Catholics run 90 percent of Irish public schools. The church, campaigning hard against passage, rang church bells twice a day over state radio and television to remind Irish voters to recite the "Angelus."

(The "Angelus" is a Catholic prayer with the well-known phrase, "Hail Mary, full of grace." Millet immortalized it in 1859 with a painting of two peasant farmers bowing their heads and folding their hands to recite it.)

"I wanted to be an equal citizen in my own country and now I am," exulted Leo Varadkar, the country's first openly gay cabinet minister, after the vote. Sister Stanislaus Kennedy, advocate for the rights of the Irish homeless, called marriage equality "a civil right and a human right."

Leading the transformation were young people--those under 35--who were youngsters when Mary Robinson fought and won the fight to decriminalize homosexuality. A few years later she became Ireland's first woman president.

The gay-wedding vote was a clear indication that the Catholic Church in Ireland is being forced into modernity by plebiscite. Contraception was illegal in Ireland until 1980. Homosexuality was not legalized until 1993. The right to divorce was granted in Ireland only in 1996.

The exceedingly wise Archbishop of Ireland, Diarmuid Martin, applauded the liberalization. He declared that the Irish "must not deny the realities." The young people empathetically did not even though most of the yes voters for gay marriage were products of Catholic schools.

Another outdated law may soon be up for a referendum: abortion. It is illegal in Ireland unless a woman's life is endangered, forcing Irish women to travel to the United Kingdom for an abortion.

But attitudes are clearly changing. Opinion polls and research show ever-increasing support for abortion.

Even the Irish politicians are now daring to support abortion in public. Niall Behan, head of the Irish equivalent of U.S. Planned Parenthood, predicts the next Irish government will hold a referendum on the anti-abortion law.

The likely outcome: repeal and another victory for freedom.

Gates prods Scouts

In another move toward freedom, former defense secretary Bob Gates has called on the Boy Scouts to end their ban on gay leadership.

Gates, now the president of the Boy Scouts of America, told executives at the national meeting: "We must deal with world as it is. If the Scouts do not change the policy, the courts will probably force them to."

Gates, an Eagle Scout, battled successfully as defense secretary to abolish the discriminatory military policy about gays: "don't ask: don't tell."

Boy Scout membership has been shrinking for decades. Ending that obsolete ban could stanch that flow.

Vatican recognizes Palestine

The Vatican joined the worldwide push for Palestinian statehood by declaring recently its recognition of Palestine as a state. Vatican recognition lends important symbolic support to a two-state solution adamantly opposed by Israeli Prime Minister Netanyahu.

Palestinian leaders called the gesture notable because of the international stature of Pope Francis. Husam Zomlot, a senior Palestinian foreign affairs official, declared: "The Vatican is not just a state. It represents hundreds of millions of Christians throughout the globe. The moral significance is vast."

As a Vatican spokesman said, the statehood endorsement counters images of Palestinians as terrorists. It is also, she said, "recognition of the Palestinian desire for coexistence and peace." That too is in line with the Francis doctrine of worldwide peace.

Mindless editors

Newspaper editors are often so puritanical they occasionally refuse to print great pictures. Such was the case with the Associated Press photographer Nick Ut who shot the magnificent story-telling photo of the Vietnamese "Napalm Girl."

The nine-year-old girl is pictured running naked down a road after being badly burned in a napalm attack in 1972. Her mouth is wide open, obviously screaming in terror, with her arms outstretched.

One lower echelon AP editor said: "We can't run the picture because she's naked." Another said: "This is a picture we can't use because she's entirely nude."

A wiser editor had the last word: the boss of the news agency. "Write a caption immediately and run it," he ordered. The photo appeared on the front page of every newspaper in America. The picture provoked anti-war protests all over the world.

The photo had not a whiff of sex. Instead, it pictured human drama and poignancy. Some editors do lack smarts.

One colleague, Professor Warren Lerude, agreed. He is a former AP Reporter.

Sparks Tribune, June 30, 2015

Puritanical NFL upholds ban
on medical marijuana

Twenty-three states and the District of Columbia have legalized medical marijuana. Four states and D.C. have legalized pot for recreational uses. But the puritanical National Football League refuses to lift the ban on marijuana.

Eugene Monroe, in a seven-year NFL career as an offensive forward, has had concussions, several shoulder injuries, ankle sprains and the terrible pounding of line play.

He uses medical cannabis to ease that chronic pain but NFL Commissioner Roger Goodell says "no" based on his own blind medical advisers. Monroe rightly castigates Goodell for that blindness. Here's how serious Monroe is: he has contributed $10,000 for research on medical marijuana and urged other players to do likewise.

Meanwhile we have the absurd Alabama law of sentencing a 75-year-old disabled veteran to prison for life for growing three dozen marijuana plants. He, too, is using cannabis to ease chronic pain, not to sell it.

But since the vet, Lee Brooker, was convicted of a felony in Florida 20 years earlier, Alabama law required a life sentence. This is a violation of the Eighth Amendment barring cruel and unusual punishment.

Ray Moore, chief justice of the Alabama Supreme Court, did not rule on the case but he called Brooker's sentence "excessive and unjustified," revealing "grave flaws" in Alabama's sentencing law.

It sure does. But it is typical of repressive Southern laws on abortion, voting rights, gays and transgenders.

Voting Rights Lose in N.C.

A federal judge, of all people, recently upheld discrimination in a North Carolina voting law.

The regressive and restrictive law cuts out same-day voter registration, pre-registration for 16- and 17-year-olds, cuts back on early voting by a week, bars counting votes outside the voters' home precinct and requires voter ID.

Judge Thomas Schroeder, a Republican appointee, admitted the law was discriminatory to black voters. Yet he concluded--incredibly--"voting is no longer a problem in North Carolina and the law does not exacerbate existing disorders."

State lawmakers said the law was necessary to reduce voter fraud. Absurd. Voter fraud is infinitesimal. The law was really designed to reduce black voting. Blacks usually vote Democratic.

Enlightened Southern Governor

In sharp contrast, an enlightened Virginia governor issued an executive order restoring voting rights to more than 200,000 felons who have served their sentences.

Virginia had been one of just four states that kept felons from voting. (The others: Florida, Iowa and Kentucky.)

Gov. Terry McAuliffe wisely said in a statement: "I want you back in society. I want you feeling good about yourself. I want you voting, getting a job and paying taxes."

Governor McAuliffe is a Democrat. He served as chairman of the Democratic National Committee from 2001 to 2005.

All Southern politicians aren't regressive.

Restrictive Abortion Laws

South Carolina has become the 17th state banning abortion after 19 weeks. It, like the other anti-abortion states, faces challenges in the federal courts.

But South Carolina is undaunted, requiring abortion clinics to get admitting privileges for doctors and banning a second-trimester procedure known as the evacuation method. Exceptions: rape and if a mother's life is in danger and a physician determines she cannot survive.

Abortion is a mother's choice but sadly the South Carolina primitives can only be deterred by the courts.

Oklahoma Makes Abortion a Felony

Another Southern state is even worse: the Oklahoma legislature passed a bill recently making abortion a felony. Doctors convicted under the law would be stripped of their medical licenses.

State Senator Nathan Dahm, who sponsored the bill, declared that pregnancy begins with conception. But Gov. Mary Fallin, a Republican, wisely vetoed the measure.

Nevertheless, Southern Crackers are relentless in their assault on Roe v. Wade.

Sparks Tribune, May 31, 2016

Shakespeare, Beethoven head my Pantheon

The following are my Immortals, the people in history who interested and fascinated me:

• Shakespeare, best playwright and poet of all time. ("Hamlet" the best play ever written.)

• Beethoven, the greatest, most profound composer ever. ("The Ninth Symphony")

• Thomas Paine, blaster of organized religion in "The Age of Reason" and revolutionist in three countries, America, Britain and France.

• Voltaire, battler of religious superstition, fanaticism and intolerance during the Enlightenment. His delightful "Candide" spoofed the view of Dr. Pangloss that this "was the best of all possible worlds." Exiled from France by Louis XV for denouncing autocratic monarchy and the myth-making Catholic Church, he spent the last 25 years of his life in Ferney, Switzerland.

• Thoreau, "Walden" ("The mass of men lead lives of quiet desperation") and "Civil Disobedience" ("Must the citizen ever for a moment resign his conscience to the legislator?")

• Oscar Wilde, witty, brilliant, learned playwright characterized by "The Importance of Being Earnest" and "The Picture of Dorian Gray."

• Jesus Christ, the first and last Christian, the most humane and understanding man who ever lived. ("He that is without sin among you, let him first cast a stone at her" (John 8:7)…"For what shall it profit a man if he shall gain the whole world and lose his own soul?" (Mark 8:36)

• Lincoln, the greatest president America ever had, wise, humorous and compassionate.

• Franklin Roosevelt, America's second best president with his progressive New Deal. Yet he was a virulent racist, keeping the strong Negro press from his White House press conferences, embracing segregation and refusing to desegregate the military.

• Joan of Arc, led the fight to drive the English from France but, betrayed by the Burgundians, was accused of heresy and dressing like a man. Put on trial, despite a magnificent defense, she was convicted and burned at the stake in Rouen. (1431)

• De Gaulle, led the free French against the Nazi occupation of Paris and freed Algeria from the French colonial yoke. (He rightly lamented: "old age is a shipwreck.")

• Orson Welles, genius, performed as Macbeth at 8, played an incomparable Falstaff in films ["Banish plump Jack and banish all the world"] and shined as the fraudulent Cagliostro in "Black Magic."

• Lenin, great founder of the Soviet Union.

• Trotsky, brains of Soviet Revolution and commander of rebel armies. Exiled from Russia by Stalin, he was murdered in Mexico by a Stalin hatchet man.

• Debs, socialist, compassionate, political prisoner jailed for denouncing U.S. entrance in World War I. As an atheist he proved that you don't have to believe in God to be ethical, moral and decent.

• Goldman, like Debs, was a sterling jailbird. A lioness of anarchy, she was sent to prison for illegally distributing information about birth control. There she won the respect and love of inmates. As prison nurse, she showed tender loving care and concern. She constantly pleaded for women's rights..

• Paul Robeson, son of an escaped slave, was a great actor and singer. But after he won the Stalin Peace Prize, life in the U.S. became intolerable so he moved to London. (Starred in Jerome Kern's "Show Boat" and wowed audiences singing "Ol Man River.")

• Solzhenitsyn, the Gulag trilogy and the classic "One Day in the Life of Ivan Denisovich." A cruel colleague squealed that he had criticized Stalin so was sent to prison in the Gulag for eight years. (The brutal dictator Stalin sold out the Soviet revolution.)

• Jack London, author of "The Call of the Wild" and "The Iron Heel," which urged a socialist revolution.

• Mencken, mocking, sardonic, vitriolic, snarled about "the swinish multitudes" of Americans who are "an ignominious mob of serfs."

• Orwell, author of "Nineteen Eight-four," one of the most influential books ever written, frequently quoted today even though he wrote it 65 years ago. In a collection of essays, "Shooting an Elephant," he attacked the British colonial empire. "Down and Out In Paris and London" described his poverty-stricken, vagabond days. His "Homage to Catalonia" recounted his fight for the Republicans in the civil war but becoming disillusioned with the lies and deceit of the communist so-called allies. "Animal Farm." This Orwell novel, scores totalitarianism.

• Dickens, a raft of good novels, including "Bleak House" and "David Copperfield" and the unforgettable Scrooge in "A Christmas Tale."

• Darwin, "The Voyage of the Beagle," visit to the Galapagos and propounder of natural selection and evolution.

• Lautrec, a troubled great painter, who gave us an intimate view of La Belle Époque.

• M.L. King battled for civil rights for African Americans, attacked the savagery of capitalism and the tremendous gap between rich and poor. Genesis 37:19, 20 says: "Behold, this dreamer cometh; let us slay him." He was, at a Memphis, Tenn., motel his dream unfulfilled.

• Malcolm X, while King wonderfully urged civil rights for African Americans, Malcolm went a step farther by urging black pride. "I'm black and I'm proud," as a popular song put it.

• Schweitzer, "Reverence for life."

- Michelangelo, the greatest artist who ever lived, his "Pieta" in the Vatican, Sistine Chapel ceiling and the huge statues of David and Moses.
- Da Vinci, second greatest artist with his magnificent painting of "The Last Supper" and paintings of "Virgin of the Rocks," "Lady in Ermine" and "Mona Lisa."
- Van Gogh, a great artist who overcame awful misery but, his mind at last deranged, he committed suicide.
- Manet, the originator of Impressionism, with great paintings such as "Luncheon on the Grass," the nude "Olympia" and "A Bar at the Folies-Bergere. (The woman keeping bar wears a sad-faced expression for the ages.)
- Rembrandt, one of the greatest painters in European art history. "The Night Watch," "The Anatomy Lesson," "Syndics of the Draper's Guild" and "Bathsheba at her Bath."
- Vermeer, produced only 34 paintings but one was the marvelous "The Girl with a Pearl Earring." Another of his interior works, the wonderful "The Milkmaid."
- Balzac wrote many novels but "Le Pére Goriot" is his best. ("Behind every great fortune there is a crime.") Buried in the famous Pére la Chaise cemetery in Paris. Old Goriot, like King Lear, loved well but not wisely.
- Rousseau's "The Social Contract" outlines a political order based on classic republicanism. "Confessions" is an autobiography and "Émile" is a treatise on the education of people for citizenship.
- Mozart, "Symphony No. 41" ("Jupiter"), quartets in homage to Haydn, "The Flute Quartet No. 1" and so much more magnificent music.
- Hugo, "Les Miserables," his book is too long with too many plots and subplots. But the struggle between the ex-convict, Jean Valjean, a remarkably good man, and the relentless pursuit of police inspector Javert, makes it a great novel.
- Gandhi in South Africa 1893-1914, preached non-

violent resistance and called the Mahatma (great soul). But he served the British Empire in South Africa, fought for the Asiatic Indians and showed little concern for blacks.

• Moliére, one of the greatest playwrights exemplified by his classic "Tartuffe," a wonderful scalding of a hypocrite.

• Primo Levi wrote the moving account of the Holocaust, "Survival in Auschwitz." The murder of six million Jews is almost an abstraction compared with Anne Frank's diary, which vividly personalizes the horror of the Holocaust.

• Mark Twain, author of Huck Finn and Tom Sawyer, stories of universal boyhood, the humorous "The Innocents Abroad" and the jollity of "The Celebrated Jumping Frog of Calaveras County."

• Poe, great writer of horror stories of ratiocination ("The Tell-Tale Heart," "The Pit and the Pendulum," "Murders in the Rue Morgue" and "The Fall of the House of Usher".) His lyric "Annabel Lee" and majestic "The Raven" make a large claim to be America's best poet.

• FitzGerald-Khayyam, translation into English of the "Rubaiyat of Omar Khayyam," captures the essence of wine, woman and song in the 101 quatrains of this great poem. Saki, cupbearer of the gods, sums up its spirit: "And in your joyous errand reach the spot / Where I made One-- turn down an empty Glass!"

• Margaret Fuller was a radical far ahead of her time in the early 20th century. Women's rights advocate, feminist pioneer, she urged jobs and education for women and called for prison reform. Socialist, writer and transcendentalist, she often visited the utopian community of Brook Farm, which stressed hard work and hard thinking (intellectual development).

• Tolstoy, wrote "War and Peace," one of the great works of literature, dealing with an aristocratic family during the French invasion of Russia. Faulkner called another of his books, "Anna Karenina," the best novel ever written.

• Chekhov, master playwright of "The Seagull," "Uncle Vanya," "Three Sisters" and "Cherry Orchard." His best story is "Ward No. 6."

• R.L. Stevenson is one of the most translated writers in the world. His works include "Treasure Island," "Kidnapped" and "Strange Case of Dr. Jekyll and Mr. Hyde." Also, don't forget his: "A Child's Garden of Verses."

• O'Neill, America's greatest playwright with such masterpieces as "Long Day's Journey Into Night," "Anna Christie," "The Iceman Cometh," "Mourning Becomes Electra" and "Ah, Wilderness."

• Dorothy Day, fought for workers, justice and humanity. She co-founded The Catholic Worker, which still publishes with positions far ahead of the Vatican. Jailed in 1917 for picketing the White House on behalf of women's suffrage.

• Dorothea Lange, her powerful photo of "Migrant Mother" and her grim picture of "The White Angel Breadline" characterized the Great Depression.

• Earl Warren, the greatest chief justice, brought so much equality to the nation by leading the court in modernizing the Constitution.

• Brandeis, the best justice the court ever had. His frequent dissents were best exemplified by the Olmstead case (1928) in which a conservative court upheld wiretapping. "Better that some criminals escape than that the government play an ignoble part...If government becomes a lawbreaker it breeds contempt for the law."

• Verdi, great opera composer: "Rigoletto," "Il Trovatore." "La Traviata" and "Aida."

• Puccini, great opera composer: "La Boheme," "Tosca," "Madame Butterfly" and "Turandot."

• Camus, "The Stranger." Meursault, about to be hung, rightly tells a shriving priest, "none of your certainties is worth a strand of a woman's hair."

• Joyce, perhaps the greatest writer who ever lived. He wrote "Dubliners" ("the awful winepress of sorrow"), "A Portrait of the Artist as a Young Man," a must read, and the often incomprehensible "Ulysses." It ends on the affirmative note of the Molly Bloom soliloquy: "Yes my mountain flower and first I put my arms around him and drew him down to me so he could feel my breasts all perfumed yes and his heart going like mad and yes I said yes I will Yes."

• Dostoyevsky, one of the world's greatest writers, "Crime and Punishment," "The Brothers Karamazov," "Anna Karenina" and "The House of the Dead," dealing with his four-year imprisonment in a labor camp.

• Zola, his excellent "Germinal" located in a suffocating mine, and the drunkard in "L'Assommoir." In an open letter, he scored the French president for anti-Semitism and wrongful imprisonment.

• Ibsen, one of the world's great playwrights: "A Doll House, (Nora Helmer as a pioneer feminist), Hedda Gabler" and "An Enemy of the People." ("The majority is never right"…"the strongest man in the world is he who stands alone.")

• Moliére, one of the greatest playwrights exemplified by his classic "Tartuffe," a delightful exposure of a hypocrite.

• Faulkner, amid all his incomprehensible garbage, we get his well written, best book: "Light in August." It is a plea for to end of racial intolerance, hatred of African Americans and their discrimination—this in a 1932 novel!

• Sartre, wrote "No Exit." ("Hell is other people.")

• Audubon who painted 436 birds. My favorite: the extinct ivory-billed woodpecker, chipped-off bark flying and bills pointed at bark beetles—action in a picture!

• Muir as a biographer phrased it: "A wonderful spirit who turned Americans into 'greenies,' people who love nature and 'the great outdoors,'

• Favorite movies, "Alice in Wonderland" (Cary Grant, Gary Cooper, W.C. Fields); "The Wizard of Oz" (Judy Garland); "Casablanca" (Humphrey Bogart, Ingrid Bergman, pianist Sam (Dooley Wilson) and inspector Claude Rains); and "Around the World in 80 Days" (Cantinflas, David Niven, Robert Newton and Shirley McLaine.)

Sparks Tribune, Jan. 12, 2016

U.S. subjugates Puerto Rico;
N.Y. Times OKs colonization

The New York Times is the world's greatest newspaper but its opinion so often is reactionary. For instance: justifying colonialism and imperialism.

A recent editorial in the Times lamented Puerto Rico's $72 billion debt to investors and $46 billion deficit in government pension funds. "It will default on payment of $2 billion in bond payments on July 1," the Times editorialized. "It desperately needs to restructure its debt."

An earlier editorial in the Times pronounced: "It's much better for Puerto Rico to be under the beneficent sway of the United States than to engage in doubtful experiments in self-government."

Beneficent sway or under the Iron Heel? In supreme irony, Puerto Rico was liberated by Spain in 1897 but promptly subjugated by America.

The Times refuses to mention what is essential for Puerto Rico: statehood. The Caribbean islanders were given U.S. citizenship in 1919 but continued to be exploited and oppressed by America.

Nelson Denis, author of "War Against All Puerto Ricans and Terror in America's Colony," documents racist, military and economic rhetoric justifying colonization.

When Spain freed Puerto Rico it guaranteed its people the right to a constitution, a legislature, power to levy tariffs, have a treasury, a monetary system and international trade. All the duties and functions of an independent state.

Actually, the U.S. today controls everything on the island: foreign relations, customs, immigration, the postal system, radio, television, military service, transportation, banking, judiciary, tariff, trading and Social Security. Doubtless the Internet and everything connected with the Digital Age too.

"The U.S. military presence in Puerto Rico is

overwhelming," Denis noted. "You can't drive five miles in any direction without passing an Army base, nuclear site or tracking station. The Pentagon controls 13 percent of the land and operates five atomic missile bases.

"Vieques island was bombed mercilessly for 62 years. From 1984 through 1998 more than 1,300 warships and 4,200 aircraft used the island for target practice.

"From the mid-1950s until 2006 the U.S. laid a red carpet from Wall Street to San Juan, Puerto Rican capital. U.S. corporations were given 10- and 20-year tax exemptions on all gross revenues, dividends, interest and capital gains.

The control was so fierce that under a U.S. law in force from 1948 to 1957 the islanders could not utter a word, sing a song, whistle a tune or say anything against the U.S. government without being subject to 10 years in prison for "seditious conspiracy."

Draconian U.S. Law

Other U.S. crimes against Puerto Rico in the past: laws prohibiting the teaching of any language except English and barring the flying of the Puerto Rican flag. However, a draconian law still in existence: the Jones Act requiring that every product that enters or leaves Puerto Rico must be carried on a U.S. ship.

The U.S. Supreme Court, with an incredible but typical reactionary ruling by nine blind justices, held in 1922 that the Constitution did not apply to Puerto Rico. It said that U.S. minimum wage laws and other federal protections and immunities were not guaranteed Puerto Ricans.

Puerto Rico's Gov. Garcia Padilla announced recently that insolvency was inevitable: it cannot pay its debts. Congress and President Obama don't care. Yet the so-called commonwealth remains under absolute U.S domination 55 years after the United Nations General Assembly declared it a sovereign nation.

Its three and one-half million people pay taxes to the United States but have no vote in presidential elections, no ballots in the Electoral College and no members in Congress. (Per capita income is extremely low, less than half that of the poorest state in the union.)

It should have been granted statehood decades ago but has always been stymied by a don't-care Congress. The deeper and unspoken reason for the stymie: Republicans fear Puerto Ricans would always elect two Democrats as U.S. senators. With the GOP and Democrats closely divided in the Senate, two more Democrats are intolerable to the GOP.

So we have a forsaken land burdened with debt but no exit, no way out. Politics rules, not fairness and justice. Drug companies and other firms absconded to Asia for cheap manufacture. Result: unemployment hovers between 12 and 14 percent.

Pedro Pierluisi, a Democrat, is Puerto Rico's non-voting delegate in the House of Representatives. He pointed out in a Times op-ed article that five million people of Puerto Rican heritage live in America.

"As conditions deteriorate, my constituents are leaving for the mainland at a rate of 50,000 a year," Pierluisi wrote. "The main reason is inequality.

"Congress routinely mistreats Puerto Rico. Federal funding for state Medicare is open-ended but capped in Puerto Rico. The only solution is statehood. Until then Puerto Ricans will remain second-class citizens."

Sparks Tribune. June 21, 2016

Rejoicing at downfall of Blatter

Power tends to corrupt and absolute power corrupts absolutely.

Lord Acton, 18th century British historian

Michel Platini, a redoubtable soccer player for French teams 35 years ago, would make an excellent replacement for Sepp Blatter, 79-year-old godfather of soccer who resigned in utter disgrace.

Pele, world soccer legend, said offensive midfielder Platini was "the brain organizing his team on the pitch, He was the best European soccer player of the 1980s." But far more to the point, Platini has successfully served as president of the prestigious Union of the European Football Association since 2007.

Adding to the shame of the Fédération Internationale de Football Association (FIFA), Blatter was re-elected to another four-year term as president. Blatter stubbornly insisted for five days after his re-election that he would not resign.

However, the firestorm overwhelmed him. He himself became the target of a federal investigation and caused global outrage at his infamy. His position as soccer dictator became untenable.

As the New York Times demonstrates time and time again, it is the best newspaper in the world. It superbly covered the latest scandal of FIFA.

The Blatter organization operated like the Mafia and international drug cartels. Its scale of corruption was beyond belief. Immense bribes were offered to get countries named host of the World Cup.

Jack Warner is the ignominious symbol of the scandal. As the Times reported in a front-page exposé: "Warner, as a committeeman from Trinidad and Tobago, shopped his ballot to the highest bidder. In 2004 a Moroccan member of the bid committee offered him $1 million. But South Africa offered a sweeter deal: $10 million. Warner voted for South Africa. It got the World Cup in 2010 and he got $10 million."

Luis Figo, former star of Barcelona and Real Madrid soccer clubs, declared: "The voting process is a plebiscite for the delivery of absolute power to one man, something I refuse to go along with."

Because of the huge profits reaped from World Cups, FIFA has become a revenue-sharing colossus that ensured Blatter the votes of scores of developing nations, overwhelming the far more important and far more powerful European and South American soccer teams.

Diego Maradona, legendary Argentina footballer, wrote: "Under Blatter, FIFA disgraced and painfully embarrassed those of us who care deeply about football."

Bribes also decided who televised matches. The sponsors of the 2014 World Cup spent millions of dollars on a corruption-riddled organization. The Corruption Four sponsors: Budweiser, Coca-Cola, Adidas and McDonalds.

Blatter's right-hand man, FIFA secretary general Jerome Valcke, made $10 million in illegal bank transactions, putting the probe close to Blatter, who has never been indicted.

The U.S. Justice Department, led by the FBI, announced indictments of 14 soccer officials and marketing executives who have corrupted the sport for two decades with blatant deals. Charges included: bribes and kickbacks in conjunction with broadcast and telecast rights to Gold Cup matches, international tournaments organized by FIFA's North American and Caribbean divisions.

Nicolás Leoz of Paraguay received bribes for two decades in exchange for awarding companies the marketing and media rights to Copa America, South America's soccer championship.

Blatter has been tone-deaf to scores of complaints during his 17-year reign. On his watch corruption was "rampant, systematic and deep-rooted," the Times editorialized. Yet he never cared what anyone thought. He ran a rogue organization.

Loretta Lynch, U.S. attorney general, spearheaded the investigation. She was so successful Le Figaro of France called her "the woman who is rocking FIFA." And in Germany, home of a soccer powerhouse, she was hailed as the "FIFA Jägerin" (hunter).

Other Times denunciations of the Blatter regime: "Appalling treatment of foreign laborers working on World Cup facilities in the blistering heat of Qatar. Hundreds of migrant World Cup workers, many from Nepal and Asian countries, have died in conditions that violated international labor laws and human rights."

FIFA should re-examine its decision to hold the World Cup in Qatar in 2022, a country with money to burn but no respect for human rights. Moreover, even FIFA's move of the games from summer to November and December provides scant relief from 120-degree heat--insane, barbarous weather for a game demanding constant running.

Blatter's FIFA has been "byzantine and impenetrable," operating behind closed doors with revenues in the past three years of $5.7 billion. He rendered the "beautiful game" ugly. Even the organization's watchdog auditor, using the initials, KPMG, did not bark. It always gave FIFA a clean slate.

Sparks Tribune, June 16, 2015

Syracuse basketball coach, Armstrong are denounced

Love of sports has been deeply engrained in me ever since I was sports editor of the Penn State student newspaper, The Daily Collegian, eons ago. But I love higher education even more than I do sports.

So I found a recent analytical story in the New York Times terribly upsetting. It revealed how Syracuse basketball coach Jim Boeheim systematically undermined the very purpose of higher education.

"Boeheim placed the desire to achieve success on the basketball court over academic integrity," an investigating committee of the National Collegiate Athletic Association reported. "Over the course of a decade academic fraud, cash payouts to players, failing to monitor the staff and lack of control prevailed."

The Syracuse chancellor promised to do everything he could "to insure events like the ones detailed in the report do not happen again."

A newspaper investigation as long as 25 years ago pointed out that the Syracuse basketball team took cash and gifts from university boosters. The team got a player's failing grade changed to make him eligible for an important game.

Boeheim built an empire. His team packed its 35,446-capacity Carrier Dome field house, earning him a salary of $1,818,661 and allowing him to bask in a heroic glow. (Boeheim's salary ranks a "mere" 23rd compared with the leader, coach Mike Krzyzewski of Duke, who earns an obscene $9,682,032.)

The infractions committee of the NCAA hit Syracuse with severe penalties: loss of 12 scholarships over the next four years, recruiting restrictions for two years and probation for five years. Boeheim also received suspension of nine games next year.

The coach got off too easy. Boeheim should have been fired. Yet he admitted no wrongdoing.

"The committee was unfair," Boeheim said. "I am disappointed with many of the findings and conclusions in the infractions report. The committee ignored the efforts I have undertaken over the past 37 years to promote an atmosphere of compliance."

Ah, atmosphere of compliance.

All across America, sports pages insist on referring to college football and basketball teams as having programs. Sports editors and writers support the grandiose rather than tell the shabby truth.

Program and programs are euphemisms, misnomers like student athletes, who are professionals training in the "minor leagues" for the big leagues. The March Madness tournament going on right now will reap the NCAA $800 million.

Major college sports build fiefdoms and make millions of dollars for universities and millions of dollars for nearby communities. But in doing so, like Boeheim, they often lose their moral compasses.

What is badly needed now: pay and unions for college athletes on major basketball and football teams. U.S. District Judge Claudia Wilken ruled last year that student athletes get paid at least $5,000 per season for rights to their names, images and likenesses. Not enough and not the last word on the matter--but a wise start.

Armstrong the doper

A Times analysis piece the same Sunday as the Boeheim story showed how the International Cycling Union (UCI) whitewashed the Lance Armstrong doping scandal.

The scathing 227-page indictment blamed the cycling governing board for a vast cover-up rather than a genuine effort to expose doping.

"Lance Armstrong was considered a veritable icon by

the institution," the report said. "A cancer survivor who helped the sport to recover and restore some credibility to UCI."

The article concluded that the "main goal was to ensure that the report reflected UCI's and Armstrong's personal conclusions."

Armstrong's career certainly sounded remarkable: cancer survivor, seven-time winner of the Tour de France, great copy for sports writers and Armstrong as a role model for thousands of cycling followers. (The three-week Tour every summer is the most prestigious bicycle race in the world.)

The report said Armstrong's immense influence compelled officials to ignore his drug use. It also enabled his lawyer secretly to write and edit an earlier version of the investigation.

As early as 2005, the French sports daily L'Equipe carried an article reporting that Armstrong tested positive for doping during his first victory in 1999. But the performance-enhancing story was buried.

In 2012 the U.S. Anti-Doping Agency exposed Armstrong's sophisticated cheating "in devastating breadth and detail." But Armstrong stoutly refused to admit he did anything wrong until his confession in 2013.

Armstrong, who repeatedly told lies to protect his storied image, ended up as a sad sack loser who made millions illicitly.

The UCI, like Boeheim, refused to admit any mistakes.

"There is a lot of things we could have done better but that is easy to say 25 years later," said Hein Verbruggen, former UCI president and target of the Armstrong cover-up. "I was criticized as a dictator and accused of being too close to Armstrong."

A feeble defense. Verbruggen was too chummy with Armstrong. And like the heads of major sports bodies, had a tendency to rule like a czar.

As for Armstrong, he was exposed as a phony like one of his many stirring quotations: "Winning is about heart, not just legs." Winning for Armstrong was all about cheating.

Sparks Tribune, March 17, 2015

Arts and Letters

Celebrating 400th birthday
of incomparable Bard

*Brush up your Shakespeare / Start quoting him now /
Brush up your Shakespeare / And the women you will
wow.*

From "Kiss Me Kate" musical based on
"The Taming of the Shrew"

Some critics of William Shakespeare's day called him
a Shake-scene, an upstart crow. One playwright of that era
described him as someone who "beautified himself with
our feathers."

The great novelist Leo Tolstoy, who should have
known better, said the Bard's greatest plays--"Hamlet,"
"King Lear" and "Macbeth"--left him with "an irresistible
repulsion and tedium."

But Shakespeare's contemporary, playwright Ben
Jonson, was far wiser. While wishing that the Bard had
"blotted a thousand" lines, Jonson described him as "not
of an age but for all time!"

Several decades after the death of Shakespeare in 1616,
poet John Dryden lauded him as having had "the largest
and most comprehensive soul."

Then in the 18th century poet Alexander Pope declared:
"every single character in Shakespeare is as much an
individual as those in life itself." And the great Samuel
Johnson, critic and lexicographer, hailed him as an author
"who invented so much and effused so much novelty" onto
the stage.

The world is justly celebrating the 400th birthday
April 23 of the Stratford lad who never went to college
but outshone every other writer who ever lived, including
many with university degrees.

Yes, Shakespeare stole many plots and characters
from other writers like Boccaccio and Plutarch. He dug

into Holinshed's Chronicles for the history of England, Scotland and Ireland. But he embroidered them into great dramas. He was not writing historically accurate accounts. He was a theatrical genius, not a dull academic.

Sales of Shakespeare books vastly outsell every book in the West except the King James Bible. His works are translated into every language in the world, including Hindi, Tamil, Bengali and Urdu.

Marlowe's "mighty line" and his use of blank verse influenced Shakespeare but he not equal the Bard. He could not match the incredible abundance of lines, characters and personalities.

Hamlet, the melancholy Dane: "How weary, stale, flat and unprofitable / Seem to me all the uses of this world!"

In the depressing "King Lear" the blinded Gloucester is told "to smell his way to Dover."

Macbeth soliloquizes: "Tomorrow, and tomorrow and tomorrow, / Creeps in this petty pace from day to day / To the last syllable of recorded time, / And all our yesterday's have lighted fools / The way to dusty death. Out, out brief candle!

"Life's but a walking shadow, a poor player / That struts and frets his hour upon the stage / And then is heard no more. It is a tale / Told by an idiot, full of sound and fury / Signifying nothing."

Othello: "farewell the tranquil mind" (Bardolators utter so often in their times of trouble.)

Shakespeare an anti-Semite? Shylock in "The Merchant of Venice: "Hath not a Jew eyes? / hath not a Jew hands, organs / dimensions, senses, affections, passions? / ...If you prick us do we not bleed?"

Fat, sack-drinking Falstaff is perhaps the greatest comic figure ever created. He says of himself: "Banish plump Jack and banish the world." Indeed!

And the drunken Toby Belch in "Twelfth Night" who

puts down the puritanical Malvolio: "Dost thou think because thou art virtuous there shall be no more cakes and ale?"

"The Tempest": "We are such stuff as dreams are made on and out little life is rounded with a sleep."

Maybe I have missed some of the reader's favorite quotes. It's inevitable amid so much Shakespearean splendor.

Robert Hurwitt, theater critic of the San Francisco Chronicle, cites the hundreds of idioms coined by Shakespeare: "brave new world," "household words," "good riddance," "catch a cold" and "it's Greek to me." And just a few of those many household words: addiction, assassination, advertisement, watchdog, puking, obscene and arch-villain.

And Shakespeare's magnificent sonnets:

No. 29: "When, in disgrace with fortune and men's eyes, / I all alone beweep my outcast state / And trouble deaf heaven with my bootless cries, / And look upon myself and curse my fate."

No. 30: "When to the sessions of sweet silent thought / I summon up remembrance of things past, / I sigh the lack of many a thing I sought...

No. 35: Here's another for Bardolators in troubled times: "No more be grieved at that which thou hast done: / Roses have thorns and silver fountains mud; / Clouds and eclipses stain both moon and sun, / And loathsome canker lives in sweetest bud."

No. 55: "Not marble nor the gilded monuments / Of princes shall outlive this powerful rhyme..."

No. 60: "Like as the waves make towards the pebbled shore, / So do our minutes hasten to their end..."

No. 116: "Let me not to the marriage of true minds / Admit impediments. Love is not love / Which alters when it alteration finds / Or bends with the remover to remove."

To sum up, Shakespeare is the world's greatest playwright, the world's greatest poet and the greatest literary gift to the world.

Sparks Tribune, July 5, 2016

Weekly outrage, cheers and jeers

British actor Benedict Cumberbatch rightly detests cellphones and cameras being punched and flashed while he is acting. The Digital Age has long since become the Insensitive and Discourteous Age.

During his recent performance of "Hamlet" at the Barbican in London, Cumberbatch was about to deliver the "To be or not to be" soliloquy when a red light flashed from the third row.

"It's mortifying," he said. "There is nothing less supportable or enjoyable."

The Barbican promptly installed devices that can detect phones and cameras during performances. Offenders will be evicted immediately.

The theater should go even further, barring cellphones and cameras. If insensitive people can't exist for a couple of hours without the evils of modernity, they shouldn't be allowed to spoil play–going for those who can.

Righto Sanders

Sen. Bernie Sanders of Vermont, Democratic candidate for president, would make tuition free for all undergraduates at public universities and colleges. Righto!

The federal government could easily pay for it just by slashing military funding. Let's have fewer wars and more social benefits from Congress.

Students and their families are going deeper into debt. The average debt after four years is $25,600. The interest rate is so exorbitant they will spend half their lives paying it off.

It hardly needs saying that more college-educated men and women will greatly improve society and aid the economy.

Larry Schwartz, in an AlterNet op-ed, wrote: "Most developed countries are appalled at the idea of burdening young people with debt for a college education and strengthening the nation. In countries like Germany, Brazil, Norway, Iceland and even Panama, public university tuition is free."

Bogus voter fraud

The New York Times reports that "many people, including the Supreme Court, have bought into the fallacious line about voter fraud. It does not exist. The real voter fraud is the Texas ID law.

Such laws are racially discriminatory and anti-voter schemes. A federal appeals court panel recently ruled unanimously that the Texas ID law had a harmful effect on black and Latino voters and therefore violates the 1965 Voting Rights Act.

Another example of how federal courts so often make sure all people are granted liberty.

Climate change gains

President Obama's clean power plan took a bold step recently against people who reject climate change, imposing nationwide limits on carbon-dioxide pollution from power plants. These plants are the source of 31 percent of America's greenhouse gas emissions.

"It will shut down hundreds of coal-fired power plants and give momentum to carbon-free energy sources like wind and solar power," the Times editorialized. "Having already set fuel efficiency standards for cars and trucks, Obama now has leverage with other nations heading into the United Nations climate-change conference in December in Paris."

Opposition to clean power comes, as expected, from the industry, Congress and the states.

Pot backing grows

Obama has the "slows" when it comes to urging

marijuana prohibition. Pot is classified as a Schedule I drug like heroin and LSD under the Controlled Substances Act.

The absurdity is manifest. Pot is an important medical need for some people. Moreover, it is no more harmful than too much alcohol. It should be removed from the prohibited list.

Four states and the District of Columbia have already made recreational use of pot legal: Alaska, Colorado, Oregon and Washington. Nevadans and Ohioans are expected to vote for legalization next year and Californians in 2017.

While Obama and Congress balk, a few states are leading the so-called leader.

Pentagon wars on journalists

The Defense Department recently released a manual outlining its interpretation of the laws of war. A hefty 1,176-page document, few Americans are likely to read it.

The Times in an editorial "reads" it for us: "The manual outlines the treatment of journalists covering armed conflicts that would make their work more dangerous, cumbersome and subject to censorship. These provisions should be repealed immediately.

"Allowing this document to stand as guidance for commanders, government lawyers and officials of other nations would do severe damage to press freedom. Authoritarian rulers around the world could point to it to show that their despotic treatment of journalists--including Americans--is in line with the standards set by the U.S. government."

Journalists are usually regarded as civilians but in the jargon of the Pentagon sometimes "unprivileged belligerents." This means they are sometimes afforded fewer protections than war combatants.

The manual ominously warns: "Reporting on military operations can be similar to collecting intelligence--or even spying."

So the military now spies on civilians and journalists.

Cuba still the enemy

The U.S. and Cuba are restoring relations. Good. Now Congress should promptly repeal the dreadful embargo and cruel sanctions.

A half-century of hostility to and coercion of Cuba not only failed to topple the Castro regime but showed how ruthless and merciless America can be.

Sparks Tribune, Aug. 25, 2015

Prof's novel rankings skewed

My contempt for academia increases with every professor's book I read.

Writing by professors is long-winded and pedantic. The professoriate never uses simple words, preferring important-sounding words like trope, template and counter-intuitive. They all have a PhD, the grand and glorious doctor of philosophy.

Typical is the book written by Daniel Burt, "The Novel 100, a Ranking of the Greatest Novels of All Time [2004]. (Burt is an English professor at New York University.)

Any ranking of books is just the viewpoint of one writer. Tastes in literature vary.

Example: Burt ranks "Finnegans Wake" by James Joyce as No. 26. That's nonsense. The book is unreadable from its first incomprehensible sentence: "riverrun, past Eve and Adam's, from swerve of shore to bend of bay, brings us by a commodious vicus of recirculation back to Howth Castle and Environs."

Burt writes approvingly of it--if you can correctly decipher the academic wording--as a "radical narrative and linguistic experiment, designing with infinite care a kind of perpetual story and interpretation generator." Yet he admits it is impenetrable. Joyce's brother, Stanislaus, rightly called it "driveling rigmarole."

But he lists Joyce's "Ulysses" third behind Cervantes' "Don Quixote" and Tolstoy's "War and Peace," calling it "one of the supreme human documents in all literature." I believe it should be No. 1

"Ulysses" recounts one day in the life of Leopold Bloom: June 16, 1904. It is sometimes enigmatic and puzzling, hard to read and hard to figure out but worth the effort.

Bloom is a Jew in predominantly Catholic Ireland, a middle-aged and middle-class canvasser for newspaper ads. The novel ends with the wonderful soliloquy by his wife, Molly Bloom, beginning and ending with the life-affirming yes.

Here's the close: "I put my arms around him yes and drew him down to me so he could feel my breasts all perfume yes and his heart was going like mad and yes I said yes I will Yes."

But Burt never mentions "Lady Chatterley's Lover" by D.H. Lawrence, not even in his second list of 100 novels. Critic Edmund Wilson evoked the truth: "the best description of sexual experience ever written." And another critic, Mark Schorer, noted: "the lyric portions comprise a great hymn to true marriage."

Burt wrongly put another great book, "One Day in the Life of Ivan Denisovich," among the second 100 novels. Solzhenitsyn's brief account of the frightful Gulag says more about mass murderer Stalin than millions of words could. The book is a tribute to fortitude and cunning in the face of dehumanizing conditions in a labor camp.

Many other Burt rankings are woefully wrong. "The Stranger" by Camus, is given 58th place. It belongs in the top 20. The main character, Meursault, grapples "with the implications of an absurd world." About to be executed, he tells a shriving priest: "Not one of your certainties is worth one strand of a woman's hair."

Burt lists Zola's "Germinal" No. 66. It is much better than that. André Gide declared it one of the 10 best novels ever written. The setting: coal mines in northern France. The struggle: underpaid workers versus predatory owners.

The miners, working under barbarous conditions, go on strike. Strike funds are soon depleted and workers' families slowly starve. Strikebreakers are brought in, killing 14 miners. It evokes tears in certain places.

"Madame Bovary" by Flaubert is a good novel but much lower than Burt's No. 7 listing. Incredibly, Burt lists "The Ambassadors" by Henry James as No. 18. James is often called America's best novelist. No, Mark Twain is. Re-read his Huck Finn.

Burt does place Melville's "Moby Dick" No. 6, roughly where it belongs. But he underrates "Oblomov" by Ivan Goncharov, putting the novel in 82nd place. Sure, Oblomov constantly sleeps and is totally uninteresting and insignificant. But it's a great ode to idleness and laziness.

The most outrageous ranking is "Nineteen eighty-four" by Orwell: No. 86. Orwell gave the language memorable words and phrases like Big Brother, thought police, doublethink, new-speak and un-person. A week seldom passes without some writer mentioning Orwell.

Almost as absurd, Burt puts Proust's "In Search of Lost Time," a long novel about remembering the past in seven parts, at No. 4. Yet he vastly underrates two American classics, the anti-war "The Red Badge of Courage" by Stephen Crane (No. 53) and the cry for socialism in "The Grapes of Wrath" by Steinbeck (No. 54). Another American Book, "To Kill a Mockingbird" by Harper Lee, is relegated to the second 100.

He omits another fine American novelist, Jack London, in both the first and second 100. His "The Call of the Wild" carries a Darwinian theme of adaption to survive as a sled dog in the Yukon. His "The Iron Heel" is a futuristic tale declaring the necessity of socialism.

Burt has one other fault: gross exaggeration. Too many novels are "existential," too many authors have "grandiosity of vision" and too many of his comments refer to books as landmarks and Bildungsroman.

I've read two-thirds of the novels on Burt's list of 100. That hardly qualifies me as an expert. But as a literary man, my judgment is as good or better than his. Nevertheless, literary readers are urged to get the book or his list on line and judge for themselves.

Salon, March 3, 2015

Rely on good film critics rather than Oscars

Much valid criticism has been hurled at the Academy of Motion Picture Arts and Sciences for ignoring African Americans and lacking diversity when it hands out Oscars. But there is a far deeper problem: the Oscars themselves.

The nominees and winners are selected by a narrow-minded and provincial group of 6,000. The group is 87 percent white, 58 percent male. Two-thirds are 60 years old or older.

About 1,100 actors, the most important branch, control the nominations, the New York Times reported. On the actor's branch, minorities are just 6 percent black, 3.5 percent Hispanic and two percent Asian.

Such a parochial group so often doesn't choose the best movies each year. One glaring example among many films meeting a similar fate: "Citizen Kane," starring, directed and co-written by Orson Welles.

It is one of a handful of greatest American movies ever made yet it did not win an Oscar when released in 1941.

"Kane" was voted the greatest film of all time by Sight & Sound magazine for five straights years. It led the list of the greatest 100 films. It has been universally praised for cinematography, music and narrative structure (innovative at the time with its overlapping dialogue).

Pauline Kael, great national film critic of the 1960s, said of "Citizen Kane": "It is more fun than any great movie I can think of. It is also a rare example of a movie that seems better today than when if first came out." Most films, alas, are what she called in a book, "Kiss Kiss Bang Bang." ("Lovie-dovie" and "shoot 'em up.")

The biographical "Kane" eviscerates newspaper tycoon William Randolph Hearst as the collector of trashy, exaggerated and sensational newspapers he was.

A.O. Scott, major film critic of the Times, rightly says:

"The Oscars are silly. Why should we suppose that 6,000 members of an insular and entitled professional association would be reliable judges of quality? A show-business oligarchy can't seriously be in the business of legislating tastes."

However, there is no chance of abolishing the Oscars but we can ignore them. In judging films I'd rather leave it to outstanding critics like Kael and Scott than to the Academy.

Nevada's Solar Bait-and-Switch

Nevada's Public Utility Commission, which regulates the state's energy market, announced in December a rate change drastic enough to kill Nevada's booming rooftop solar market and drive providers out of the state.

The new tariffs will gradually increase until they triple monthly fees that solar users pay for the electric grid and cut by three-quarters users' reimbursements for feeding electricity into it.

This was pointed out recently in an op-ed column in the New York Times. It was written by Jacques Leslie, author of "Deep Water: the Epic Struggle over Dams, Displaced People and the Environment."

"The 17,000 Nevada residents who were lured into solar purchases by state-mandated one-time rebates of up to $23,000 discovered they were victims of a bait-and-switch," Leslie wrote.

"They made the deals assuming that, allowing for inflation, their rates would stay constant over their 20- to 30-year contracts. Instead, they face the prospect of paying much more for electricity than if they had never made the change even though they're generating almost all their electricity themselves."

This is obviously unfair. Here's why: two of Nevada Governor Sandoval's closest advisers, Pete Ernaut and Greg Ferraro, are NV Energy lobbyists.

It's government by cronies.

False Feminists

No one expects politicians to be straight shooters. But when two purported women's libers, Gloria Steinem and Madeleine Albright, engage in gender politics they become crooked shooters.

Steinem and Albright recently endorsed Hillary Clinton for president solely because she would be the first woman commander in chief. At the same time they rebuked young women who support Sanders.

Being a woman is not enough. Clinton is the same old Establishment figure President Obama and most presidents have been. Her election would hardly be a revolution Steinem and Albright are proclaiming.

Clinton's real revolutionary opponent is Bernie Sanders. He stands for democratic socialism. He is espouses real change, not the dreary U.S. politics as usual. His platform would benefit woman of all ages.

A perfect example: Clinton opposes universal health care, declaring it would burden middle-class families and put American health insurance at risk by dismantling every major health-care institution.

On the contrary, Sanders says. He calls it the "axis" of his campaign. He wants Medicare for all, a blessing most European nations have.

Sparks Tribune, Feb. 16, 2016

Youth jail ban sought

Seattle is one of most progressive cities in America, constantly confronting musty ideas, long-festering problems and seeking betterment of its citizens.

The latest example: the Seattle City Council unanimously passed a resolution resolving to end the jailing of young lawbreakers. The council seeks to cut off the "school-to-prison pipeline" by finding alternatives to incarceration.

"This is a big win for the campaign by EPIC (Ending the Prison Industrial Complex)," Reagan Jackson commented in a Truthout article. "EPIC is leading the fight against the King County (Seattle) plan to build a $210 million juvenile detention center.

"The organization hopes to redirect funding from the mass incarceration of youth and toward community-based prevention, intervention and diversion programs and services."

EPIC doesn't know how the goal will be reached but hopes to find out by holding community meetings. The aim: not to punish anyone for law-breaking but rather to work with the person who committed the crime and its victim for a satisfactory solution.

Offenders are still accountable for their crimes but given a chance to rectify them. Jerrell Davis, Seattle artist and activist, says:

"When we talk about detention and no incarceration people are askance but jailing doesn't work. It doesn't rehabilitate them. It doesn't humanize them. Recidivism is 60 percent. People go back to prison for the same crime they went in for."

The United States has the largest prison population in the world, 2.5 million. Seattle's "restorative justice" program may be a solution.

From last to first

Oh, my, how things have changed on the cannabis battlefront. A press release from the recent District of Columbia state fair boasted: "For the first time ever we're hosting a contest for local pot growers to show off their finest plants and buds."

D.C. voted to legalize marijuana earlier this year. So Jim Hightower, vox populi (Latin: voice of the people) columnist, asks why not celebrate pot at state fairs? He notes that they already hold contests for best home brew, best ice cream, best pickles, best compost and best floral arrangements.

Progress. From demonization of the weed to legalization and celebration at state fairs!

NRA rules Congress

Every time the country endures the frequent mass shootings the welkin rings with cries for gun controls.

The outcry is prompted by the need for stronger gun controls. But the National Rifle Association doesn't care. It forbids the mildest gun controls. That's why a craven Congress does too.

The matter soon dies down until the next mass shooting. But that, too, will soon die out. Ad nauseam.

A Republican pollster found out in 2012 that 87 percent of gun owners support such a simple matter as background checks for all gun purchases.

No matter. The NRA, with 4.5 million members, always gets what it wants.

'Greyhound therapy'

Nevada will pay dearly for callously dumping homeless former mental patients in San Francisco with one-way bus tickets.

The state agreed to pay $400,000 to settle a "Greyhound therapy" lawsuit that involved getting rid of 24 men from a Las Vegas psychiatric hospital, Nevada's largest health facility.

Newspaper articles in the Sacramento Bee and San Francisco Chronicle exposed the nefarious practice. The patient-dumping toll: 1,500.

Columnist blasts Israel

Writing in the October Progressive magazine, Dave Zirin, premier sports journalist, scores Israel for its dreadful treatment of the Palestinian soccer team.

"Its players have been arrested, held in solitary confinement and killed," Zirin writes. "They also have been unable to attend international tournaments because of checkpoints, raids and other harassment."

Palestinians in the West Bank and Gaza "absolutely love basketball, too," he writes. "But eight National Basketball Association players rode on anti-union rightwing zealot Sheldon Adelson's airplane to Israel--a trip organized by the NBA's only Israeli player, Omri Casspi."

Zirin denounced the slogan the "NBA cares": "In the hands of Sheldon Adelson, NBA players became pawns of an exclusionary agenda aimed at marginalizing an entire people."

Vive la Palestine!

Sparks Tribune, Nov. 3, 2015

Grammar book by
journalism professor fails badly

The Ultimate Writing Guide for Students
By Mignon Fogarty
Scholastic, 282 pages, 2011

All writers need a demanding editor no matter how skilled and experienced they are as writers.

This is especially true of the book written by Professor Mignon Fogarty, self-designated "grammar girl" who teaches in the journalism school at the University of Nevada, Reno.

To begin with, the book is poorly written and two-thirds longer than it needs to be. It is too cutesy, school girlish and even childish. It is repetitious. The titles of topics are sometimes wrong and pretentious. The book is loaded with pop grammar quizzes. It is packed with this kind of silly heading: "THE COLON: I CAN'T WAIT TO READ WHAT COMES NEXT."

The grammar girl is wrong when she suggests this word arrangement: "I loved the movie, said Squiggly." It should be subject predict. (Squiggly said.)

The commaitis here is woeful. It may be considered grammatically correct to write "he ate apples, peaches, and oranges," as Fogarty advises, but the second comma is unnecessary. Only stuffed-shirt newspapers like the New York Times and old-fashioned editors insist on the second comma. Ditto: "Squiggly ran to the forest, but Aardvark chased squirrels." The comma is unneeded.

Should you capitalize the first word after a colon? Fogarty says it's a matter of style. As a grammarian she should be more emphatic, not saddling everyone with stodgy Times style.

"Squiggly was fixated on something: chocolate." She says a semi-colon should replace the colon. She's wrong.

A semi-colon is obsolete and should be rarely used except in a long series of phrases. As Kurt Vonnegut put it: "All they do is show that you've been to college."

The book gets tedious with constant explanatory sentences starring Squiggly and Aardvark. Like nearly all writers, speakers and lecturers, she grossly overuses "of courses" when the of course is obvious. ("Of course, a participial phrase describes the closest noun.") We get Squiggly finding green Easter eggs with a kid's "yuck" appended to Fogarty's example.

With all its many faults, the book does have good advice for students and veteran writers as well. Examples:

- Better to start a sentence with a figure rather than write the cumbersome: "Twelve thousand eight hundred and forty-two" as is required in "correct" grammar.

- Write WHO rather than the unnecessary W.H.O.-style used by the Times. All anachronisms should be spelled out on first reference: World Health Organization. Exception to the rule: the well-known FBI and CIA. (The Times is guilty of running things like FEI in a news story on first reference, leaving most readers mystified.)

- Use explanation marks sparingly. "With the explanation point, less is certainly more," Fogarty writes. Certainly is unneeded in the architect Mies van der Rohe maxim, "Less is more."

- Use of a hyphen is essential between compound adjectives: "The long-term deal." But it is often used incorrectly. Some ungrammatical editor put the hyphen in Melville's "Moby-Dick."

- Join a prefix to a word that must be capitalized: anti-American, T-shirt and 100-foot.

- "I couldn't care less" is correct, not "I could care less."

- Take out comma in this sentence: "Do I hear a waltz?,"

- "He went to town, because he needed groceries." Take out the comma although sticklers will insist on the old-fashioned way.

Editors don't rout clichés that appear every day in newspapers. Everything is an icon or iconic. Columnists too often write the word "well" as in "Scott Feldman is the reincarnation of Bob Gibson without, well, cheating."

Ever since the "Casablanca" movie we often see printed the cliché "round up the usual suspects." Another dreadful cliché after every shooting spree or disaster: horrific. And "new normal," whatever that means.

This is hardly the only how-to-write-well book that is flawed. For example: some grammar guides tell you never to end a sentence with a preposition. That's an absurd archaism. Language changes, lives and grows decade by decade.

One grammar book urges you to say "It is I," which was correct yesteryear but far better today to say "It is me." Ben Zimmer, Wall Street Journal copy editor, finds growing acceptance of they as a singular pronoun. "It is better usage than the clunky he or she or he/she," he writes.

Critical editors are particularly needed for books written by academics. The authors might be brilliant scholars but they have never learned to write. The professors use words that obfuscate rather than elucidate with such words as: template, post-modern, bell curves, meta-concepts, normalization, literary Marxism, cognitive psychology, Skinnerism psychology, tropes, generic reader and coherence connector.

The New York Times and the Reno Gazette-Journal of Nevada are terribly guilty about running 50- and 75- word sentence in stories and columns.

The Gazette-Journal prints a column about the Discovery Museum but never tells where it is. That's what happens when papers fire real editors and are left with story shufflers who know nothing about editing. Papers don't care about readers--just their ever-swelling bottom lines.

As a matter of fact, demanding editors are needed for every book published. So all editors might consider getting the Fogarty book despite its many foibles.

Sparks Tribune, May 3, 2016

Three wonderful Xmas stories

Journalism students at the University of Nevada, Reno, used to find me forbidding and intimidating. It's as if I were one of those newspaper city editors of yesteryear-- crusty, brusque and mean.

One such city editor was Charles Chapin of the New York Evening World in the late 19th century. He boasted that he had fired 108 reporters, including the son of the great Joseph Pulitzer. Chapin was so hated in the newsroom that when he called in sick one day famed reporter Irvin Cobb growled: "Let's hope it's nothing trivial."

But, no, I am hardly a Chapin throwback. What few UNR students know is that beneath my demanding, hard-shell exterior, is guy who is all mush.

I wax particularly sentimental at the Yuletide, reading my three favorite Christmas stories, the beginning of Luke 2, the start of Dickens' "A Christmas Carol" and H.L. Mencken's "Christmas Story."

Luke 2 is not my favorite biblical passage. John 8:3-13 is. Those verses sum up the essence of Jesus.

John relates how the scribes and Pharisees brought to Jesus a woman "taken in adultery, in the very act." They argued that Moses in the law commanded stoning for such an offense. Jesus replied: "He that is without sin among you, let him first cast a stone at her." The accusers, "convicted by their own conscience," departed one by one.

(Read the King James Version published in 1611. It is literature. Modern translations may be more understandable and more accurate but they lack the poetry and majesty of the KJV.)

Luke 2:1-20 is a marvelous account of the birth of Christ. Mary is "great with child," not the prosaic pregnant as in modern versions. And then: "a multitude of the heavenly host praising God and saying glory to God in the highest and on earth peace, good will toward men."

My next favorite, the Dickens classic. One of my book shelves is full of Dickens. The book with "A Christmas Carol" is discolored and torn at the base of the spine after decades of being pulled from the shelf.

The opening delights me no matter how many times I have read it. Scrooge is as "solitary as an oyster"..."No beggars implored him to bestow a trifle"...Christmas? "Bah! Humbug!" He declares that "every idiot who goes about with 'Merry Christmas' on his lips should be boiled with his own pudding and buried with a stake of holly through his heart."

When his nephew wishes him a Merry Christmas, Scrooge replies: "What right do you have to be merry? You're poor enough."

When two visitors ask for a donation for the poor, Scrooge replies starkly: he will give nothing. He cruelly adds that if people want to die they should do so in order "to decrease the surplus population." Then Scrooge "took his melancholy dinner in his usual melancholy tavern." Old. Alone. Bitter.

Ah, the Mencken story. HLM was vitrolic, acerbic, caustic, mocking, mordant, sardonic and iconoclastic. He snarled about "the swinish multitudes." He declared that "one horse laugh is worth a thousand syllogisms."

"No one ever went broke underestimating the intelligence of the American people," he declared. Moreover, Americans were an "ignominious mob of serfs and goose-steppers who live in a land of abounding quackery."

HLM was the great crusader against nonsense, a disturber of the peace. He hooted at the absurdities of boobus Americanus, his invented Latin. It sometimes seems that nothing pleased him excerpt Beethoven and German beer. But Christmas did.

Mencken reveals a tender side in his wonderful Xmas tale. It is quintessential HLM but with a twist. His "Christmas Story" was first printed in The New Yorker in

1944. Then the story was handsomely illustrated by Bill Crawford and published by Knopf as a little book in 1946.

Fred Ammermeyer, a flaming infidel who sends Baltimore clergymen the anti-religious "The Age of Reason" by Thomas Paine, is determined that the waterfront derelicts celebrate Christmas with plenty to eat and drink and to watch rousing entertainment--without any of the usual holy roller calls for repentance.

So the ne'er-do-wells ate and drank with gusto. But once satiated, the bums reverted to mission piety. They began singing hymns like "Throw Out the Lifeline," "Where Will You Spend Eternity?" and "Wash Me and I Shall Be Whiter Than Snow."

Soon the derelicts were "beating time with their beer glasses on the tables and tears were trickling down their noses." Suddenly, a bum arose and in "a quavering, boozy, sclerotic" voice launched into a confession.

"Friends," he began, "I just want to tell you what these good people have done for me, how their prayers saved a sinner who seemed past all redemption. Friends, I had a good mother who brought me up under the influence of the Word.

"But in my youth my sainted mother was called to heaven so my poor father took to rum and opium. Then I was led by the devil into the hands of wicked men—and, yes, wicked women, too."

This was too much for Ammermyer and his friend, a police lieutenant. They had been happily watching the men enjoy a Yule party without piety. But, alas, they had to slouch off in disgust at the sad turn of events.

The next day the lieutenant encountered Ammermeyer on a Baltimore street and sadly lamented: "Well, what could you expect from them bums? They have been eating mission handouts for so long they can't help it. Think of all that good food wasted! And all that beer! And all those cigars!"

Sparks Tribune, Dec. 22, 2015

Oscar Wilde: genius personified

Out of the depths have I cried unto thee, O Lord.
                    Psalms 130:1, sung in Handel's
                    glorious oratorio, "Messiah."

Brilliant. Witty. Epigramist. Great conversationalist. Playwright. Short-story writer. Novelist. Poet. Essayist. Social critic. Lecturer. Book reviewer. Journalist. Magazine editor. Classicist. Scholar. Dandy. Aestheticist. Individualist. Profound. Humane.

That was Oscar Wilde, one of the greatest multi-faceted geniuses ever to have graced the planet.

He reached the height of fame in 1895 with his celebrated play in London, "The Importance of Being Earnest." It featured two characters "bunburying" who switched personas between city and country in order to escape Victorian social mores.

He wrote the play, "Salome," in French but England refused it a performance license because biblical themes were taboo. Later Richard Strauss turned it into an opera with its erotic "Dance of the Seven Veils" and stunning image of the head of John the Baptist "served" on a platter.

Wilde's novel, "The Picture of Dorian Gray," blended themes of decadence, duplicity and beauty. His essay, "The Soul of Man Under Socialism," rips society: "Democracy means bludgeoning of the people by the people" and "that monstrous and ignorant thing, public opinion."

But all his brilliance, fame and glory crashed in tragedy: three trials hinging on homosexuality and libel, sentence to two years of hard labor in prison and exile in France.

"The love that dare not speak its name" was considered a "gross indecency" in Victorian Britain. But the real indecency was the conviction and jailing of an innocent man and a magnificent spirit.

Wilde's friends advised him not to file suit for libel but

his poor judgment prevailed. It was the beginning of his tragic end. Wilde writes about it and Jesus with truth and wisdom in "De Profundis":

• "How slowly time goes with those of us who lie in prison"…"The supreme vice is shallowness"…"To the artist, expression is the only mode under which he can conceive of life at all''… "Shakespeare, the most purely human of all the great artists."

• "Out of the carpenter's shop at Nazareth had come a personality infinitely greater than any made of myth and legend"…" 'He that is without sin among you let him first cast a stone at her.' Jesus said. It is worthwhile living to have said only that."

• "Mary Magdalene, when she sees Christ, breaks an alabaster vase that one of her seven lovers gave her and pours the sweet-smelling spices over his tired, dusty feet. That moment sits forever in paradise with the biblical Ruth and Dante's Beatrice."

• "There were Christians before Christ but none since"…"the spirit of Christ is not in the churches."

• "Prison conditions are intolerable: the plank-board bed, the loathsome food, the hard ropes shredded into oakum until one's fingers grow dull with pain, the menial duties with which each day begins and ends, the harsh orders that routine seems to necessitate, the dreadful prison clothing that makes sorrow grotesque to look at and the silence, solitude and the shame."

• "When I was brought down from prison, handcuffed between two policemen, a gentleman gravely raised his hat to me. A large crowd was hushed into silence by an action so fine and so simple. Men have gone to heaven for smaller things than that."

In letters to the Britain's Daily Chronicle, Wilde laments that a prison warden was fired because he gave sweet biscuits to a starving child.

He remarks: "What is inhuman in life is officialdom.

168

It is supposed that because a thing is the rule it is right. Justices and magistrates generally are an ignorant class."

On an upbeat note, Wilde observes that the "prisoners are usually extremely kind and sympathetic toward each other." He quotes Carlyle approvingly about "the silent charm of human companionship."

And he is "struck by the singular kindness and humanity of Warder Martin when he spoke to me and other prisoners. Kind words mean much in prison."

Wilde also relates prison sorrow in his poem, "The Ballad of Reading Gaol": "And alien tears will fill for him / Pity's long broken urn, / For his mourners will be outcast men / And outcasts always mourn." These lines are engraved on Wilde's tomb at the Père Lachaise cemetery in Paris.

Other memorable lines:

"I never saw a man who looked / With such a wistful eye / On that little patch of blue / Which prisoners call the sky"..."And twice a day the chaplain called / And left a little tract"..."And bitter wine on a sponge / was the savor of remorse (Jesus).

"A year whose days are long"..."Every stone one lifts by day / Becomes one's heavy heart by night"..."the fetid breath of living death"... "Something was dead in each of us / And what was dead was hope."

Reading assignment for next week: "De Profundis" and "The Ballad of Reading Gaol."

Sparks Tribune, Oct. 13, 2015

Supreme Court

Scalia sees democracy's end

Justice Antonin Scalia is an unbelievably retrograde thinker. He constantly dissents angrily in cases dealing with gay rights.

Consider two cases:

• In Lawrence v. Texas, (2003) the Supreme Court invalidated a Texas statute banning homosexual relations: "Today's opinion is the product of a court, which is the product of a law-profession culture, that has signed on to the homosexual agenda," Scalia wrote. "It eliminates the moral opprobrium traditionally attached to homosexual conduct.

"Many Americans do not want homosexuals in their businesses, as scoutmasters and as teachers. The court is oblivious to the fact that homosexuals are not in the mainstream."

• Obergefelle v. Hodges (2015): The Supreme Court validated gay marriage just as Scalia predicted in his Lawrence dissent. "He vented even more than his usual anger in the Hodges decision," 7th Circuit District Judge Richard Posner observed in an opinion piece in the New York Times.

"There is no principled basis for distinguishing child molesters from homosexuals since both are minorities," Scalia told Georgetown law students. "Moreover, the protection of minorities should be the responsibility of legislatures, not courts."

He ended on a note of doom: "Obergefelle marks the end of democracy in the United States. It means the people are subordinate to a Supreme Court committee of nine unelected lawyers."

He argued in Obergefelle that the Supreme Court should get out of the business of deciding the constitutionality of state statutes or laws of Congress. He told students at Rhodes College in Memphis, Tenn., the Obergefelle decision means the Supreme Court can do whatever it wants."

Whew! It is hard to know where to begin a rebuttal to Scalia's tirade.

Despite the fact that the Supreme Court often makes wrong decisions, it is indisputable that it is essential to rule on the fairness and justice of legislation. Although the legislatures and Congress often pass bad statutes and laws, a legal body is needed to determine their constitutionality.

A good example is a recent ruling of the U.S. Court of Appeals for the Ninth Circuit that was the basis of a front-page story in the Sparks Tribune. The court ruled that the Tucson, Ariz., city council election system was constitutionally flawed because in primaries voters choose nominees by wards but in general elections the entire population of Tucson can vote.

This is hardly an earthshaking case. But the circuit court was right to call the system a violation of the Equal Protection Clause of the 14th Amendment. (Reno and Sparks city councils in Nevada have the same unconstitutional systems.)

Clearly, the Supreme Court must decide the constitutionality of such legal disputes.

Scalia also showed his ignorance during a recent argument on an affirmative-action case before the Supreme Court. He declared that "some black students would benefit from being at a lower-track school" instead of the Texas flagship university in Austin. He suggested that some of those students "are being pushed ahead in classes too fast for them."

U.S. Sen. Harry Reid of Nevada promptly denounced Scalia's racist rhetoric.

"The idea that African American students are intellectually inferior to other students is despicable," Reid said. "It's a throwback to a time that America left behind half a century ago.

"That Justice Scalia could present such an uninformed idea shows just how out of touch he is with the values of this nation today. An African American student has the same potential to succeed in an academic environment as any other student."

Scalia relies on "original intent" in the Constitution about matters the Founders never thought of nor heard of. He would do America a favor by resigning from a role he is totally unfit for.

Sparks Tribune, Dec. 29, 2015

Death penalty,
solitary confinement challenged

Among its flurry of end-of-term decisions, the Supreme Court inhumanely approved execution drugs that cause excruciating pain.

The vote in the case, Glossip v. Gross, was 5-4 with swingman Justice Kennedy voting with the conservatives, Chief Justice Roberts and Justices Scalia, Thomas and Alito.

Writing the majority opinion, Alito said the three death row inmates who sought to bar the use of the drugs failed to make their case about painfulness nor suggest any preferable method of execution.

But Justice Breyer in dissent said it was time to discuss a larger issue: "Rather than try to patch up the death penalty's legal wounds, I would ask for a full briefing on a more basic question: whether the death penalty violates the Constitution. It is highly likely that executions violate the Eighth Amendment bar to cruel and unusual punishment."

Not unlikely. It is cruel. All civilized countries--except the uncivilized United States--have abolished the death penalty. Thirty-one states and the federal government cling to executions.

Breyer added in his 48-page dissent packed with charts and maps: "Long delays between death sentences and executions may themselves violate the Eighth Amendment. Innocent people have been executed. Death row exonerations are frequent. Death sentences are imposed arbitrarily and the criminal justice system is warped by racial discrimination and politics."

In his learned dissent, joined by Justice Ginsburg, Justice Breyer said there is scant reason to believe the death penalty deters murder. Besides, the death penalty is unreliable. More than 150 prisoners sentenced to death since 1973 have been exonerated.

Breyer concluded that America's criminal system is broken.

Yet on this highly important judicial matter, Justice Scalia described it as: "gobbledygook." He mocked Breyer, calling him just another in a long line of death-penalty abolitionists. He deserves impeachment for that opinion, let alone his numerous horrendous, unjudicial opinions.

In another case, Davis v. Ayala, Kennedy declared prolonged solitary confinement particularly brutal. He cited the case of Hector Ayala who has been on California's death row for 25 years.

"His windowless cell is no larger than a typical parking spot where he is confined for 23 hours a day," he wrote. "In the one hour he is allowed outside in the prison courtyard, he has little opportunity to interact with anyone."

Kennedy was right. Yet Justice Thomas called Ayala's "accommodations far more spacious than the four people he murdered now lie in." That's a blog post, as the New York Times put it, not a judicial opinion.

Kennedy quoted a character in the Dickens novel, "A Tale of Two Cities," Dr. Manette, who spent 20 years in isolation in the Bastille. Even though Manette had his beloved cobbler's bench and tools, he lost his mind.

"The Europeans today have a far better system than the United States does," Kennedy pointed out. "Even the most recalcitrant prisoners mingle frequently, having constant human contact."

He concluded by quoting another writer, Dostoyevsky, in "The House of the Dead": "The degree of civilization in a society can be judged by entering its prisons."

Let cameras in

It is long past the time for the Supreme Court to allow cameras in its courtroom.

C-Span has been televising Congress since 1979. Some federal courts allow cameras in their courts. But the

Supreme Court acts as if it is too sacred an institution to allow the intrusion of such a "modern contraption."

The court keeps throwing out bogus arguments: "we're different," cameras may promote grandstanding by lawyers and justices, and the public will not understand the proceedings.

"These excuses are condescending and unconvincing," the New York Times rightly editorialized. "But the day is coming when new leaders of the court will permit cameras."

Let's hope so. Americans are entitled to see "live" the decisions that deeply affect their lives.

Redistricting commission OK'd

The Supreme Court ruled that Arizona voters were entitled to create a redistricting commission rather than have partisan politicians draw the lines.

Twelve states have adopted independent commissions to redraw district lines rather than have the pols draw the lines for partisan advantage.

Justice Ginsburg wrote the 5-4 decision joined by Justices Kennedy, Breyer, Sotomayor and Kagan.

As usual in America, fair and decent policies are mighty slow to catch on.

Abortion reprieve

The U.S. Supreme Court allowed 10 Texas abortion clinics to reopen temporarily while the justices consider whether to hear an appeal on a decision effectively ordering them to close.

Planned Parenthood and advocates of abortion rights praised the stay of an appellate court order and said they were confident the justices would hear the case.

Anti-choice politicians in the South, like the ones in Texas, are pushing lawmakers to close clinics that provide safe and affordable clinics for abortions.

Sparks Tribune, July 28, 2015

Abolish death penalty

The death penalty is a revolting butchery, an outrage inflicted on the body and mind.
Albert Camus in "Reflections on the Guillotine"

The death penalty has no place in the 21 Century.
Ban Ki-moon, United Nations Secretary-General

The Supreme Court has been fussing about the death penalty since 1972 but refuses to declare it permanently unconstitutional.

It argues about the constitutionality of lethal injections, questions the execution of a man with an IQ of 70, squabbles about executing the insane, discusses the constitutionality of the death penalty for those who murdered before they were 18 and wonders if the proven guiltless should be executed.

But as Susanne Dumbleton writes in Truthout: "It is time to stop pretending a value-centered democracy can execute people and still honor a commitment to the dignity of the individual regardless of who that person is or what that person has done."

Last year a federal district judge, Cormac Carney, took a wise step where his highest court brethren fail the wisdom test. Carney called the death penalty "dysfunctional, random, devoid of penological purpose and unconstitutional."

The New York Times rightly complained in an editorial that some states permit the death sentence in "a process warped by injustice and absurdity." Examples:

• Florida allows a judge to impose a death sentence and does not require that the jury be unanimous in voting for execution. Primitive Alabama permits a judge to overrule a jury verdict of life in prison with a death sentence.

Alabama judges imposed death sentences 101 times after the jury voted for life.

The craven U.S. Supreme Court declined to hear a challenge to the outrageous Alabama law in 2013. Justice Sonia Sotomayor dissented over denial of certiorari, pointing out that Alabama judges are elected so they naturally "succumb to political pressures." The Alabama law undermines "the sanctity of the jury's role in our system of criminal justice," she wrote.

Chief Justice Roberts talks about "evolving standards of decency." The truth is the Supreme Court has not evolved far enough. As the Times editorialized:

"Until capital punishment is abolished, the United States will remain a notorious exception in a world that has largely rejected state-sanctioned killing. The Florida and Alabama jury laws are only one more proof of the moral disgrace of capital punishment in this country."

As the great "people's justice," Louis Brandeis, said while dissenting in a 1932 case: "We must be ever on our guard lest we erect our prejudices into legal principles." The death penalty majority should heed the Brandeis wisdom instead of sticking to its ancient prejudices.

Even the bloody ruler Robespierre during the French revolutionary Reign of Terror proposed abolition of the death penalty. He called capital punishment "base assassination, punishing one crime by another."

The death penalty is no deterrence to murder. But it is unjust, arbitrary, immoral and racist. A humanistic Supreme Court would ban it.

Unfortunately, there will always be people on the court like Justice Antonin Scalia, an originalist, who argues that justices must look to the intentions of the Framers.

"The Fifth Amendment clearly permits the death penalty and is not a cruel and unusual punishment prohibited by the Eighth Amendment," he proclaims. Execution is cruel and unusual punishment. The Fifth Amendment, written in 1787, reads: "No person shall...be deprived of life... without due process of law." That hardly meets the test of an evolving sense of decency.

As far back as Furman in 1972 the Supreme Court put a hold on the death penalty in three cases, calling the scheduled executions unconstitutional and "cruel and unusual punishment" in violation of the Eighth Amendment. Regrettably, the court reinstated the monstrosity in 1976.

Linda Greenhouse in a New York Times column wrote that the Supreme Court needs a bold justice today "to point the way to freeing the court--and the rest of us--from the death penalty."

Harry Blackmun was one such bold justice for a former court, declaring in a 1994 case: "I no longer shall tinker with the machinery of death."

Former Justices William Brennan and Thurgood Marshall also believed the death penalty was unconstitutional. They were right. The death penalty is murder by the state.

More women on the court would be a step toward abolition. Justices Ruth Bader Ginsburg, Sonia Sotomayor and Elena Kagan, the three women on the court, are anti-death penalty. Eventually they will lead a court majority to Jane Austen's "Sense and Sensibility."

Sparks Tribune, April 7, 2015

Supreme Court spreads misery

"Few institutions have inflicted greater suffering on more Americans than the U.S. Supreme Court." So writes Ian Millhiser in a new book entitled "Injustices." His subtitle elaborates: "The Supreme Court's History of Comforting the Comfortable and Afflicting the Afflicted."

His scathing indictment tells how the court routinely commits two grievous "sins" against the Constitution: embracing "limits on the government's ability to protect the most vulnerable in society while refusing to enforce rights enshrined in the Constitution."

As a result, the court is "one of the most powerful and most malign institutions in American history."

Millhiser, Senior Fellow of the Center for American Progress and editor of Think/Progress/Justice, relates Supreme Court history from the viewpoint of everyday people, not the pro-business, pro-corporation, pro-wealthy and pro-powerful so prevalent in its bleak history.

Since its inception the justices have allowed children to toil in coal mines, agreed to forcing Americans into camps because of their race and ruled that a woman could be sterilized against her will by state law. (Justice Oliver Wendell Holmes wrote the 1927 "eugenics" opinion in Buck v. Bell, declaring that "three generations of imbeciles are enough.")

The court served as midwife to Jim Crow and busted unions. Three constitutional amendments provided equal rights to freed slaves but the court largely destroyed them.

Millhiser calls the Warren Court the most progressive in history but its ruling are now being "repealed" by the Roberts Court. That nefarious body has struck down laws like the Voting Rights Act and campaign financing regulations that preserve integrity in democracy. It ignores constitutional safeguards against voter suppression laws and gerrymandering.

It declined to hear an appeal of a Wisconsin law requiring voters to provide photo ID. Proponents of the law say it is necessary to combat voter fraud. Voter fraud is non-existent. The real intent is to reduce the Democratic vote.

As a federal trial court judge wrote: the Wisconsin law would "deter or prevent more than 300,000 registered voters who lack ID from voting and would disproportionally affect black and Latino voters."

The Roberts Court ruled in 2010 that money was speech, meaning that the Koch brothers have a far, far more powerful First Amendment than nearly all Americans. But it just rightly ruled that states may prohibit candidates for state courts from asking for campaign funds.

"Judges are not politicians," Chief Justice John Roberts said. No, but Supreme Court justices are.

Gerrymandering, drawing election districts for partisan advantage, is blatant discrimination and hence unconstitutional. But not to the Roberts Court. It allows districts to be drawn in bizarre shapes that greatly diminish the number of Democratic seats in states and in Congress.

In oral argument recently, the court was divided on the issue of gay marriage. The pivotal justice, Anthony Kennedy, argued both sides. On the one hand, he called "the social science, the values and perils of same-sex marriage, too new." On the other, he expressed qualms about excluding gay couples from marriage, "having an equality and dignity that cannot be denied."

Whatever Scotus rules, gay marriage is a fait accompli. Thirty-six states and the District of Columbia have made it legal. Sixty-one percent of Americans approve of same-sex unions.

After a court in Hawaii ruled in 1993 that the state's constitution permitted gay marriage, state legislators stampeded to make it illegal. Today the issue is so moot that many gay-marriage foes fall back lamely on the Bible.

(Leviticus: 18:22, "Thou shall not lie with mankind as with womankind.") [KJV]

Justice John Paul Stevens, dissenting in a 1986 decision upholding the Georgia anti-sodomy law, declared: "The fact that the governing majority in a state has traditionally viewed a particular practice as immoral is not sufficient reason for upholding a law prohibiting it."

Stevens displayed new thinking 28 years ago. New thinking beats a millennium of old thinking. The Roberts Court majority represents old thinking, mossbacks supporting discrimination and denying equal protection of the laws to gays and lesbians.

As for old thinking, the Roberts Court has danced around the death penalty for years, wondering if a botched lethal-injection execution is constitutional. Yet the court refuses to take the new-thinking action that civilized nations have: abolish the death penalty. Neither is President Obama civilized. He opposes abolition of capital punishment.

One big case remains for decision this spring: the Affordable Care Act (Obamacare). It is a frivolous suit concocted by a rightwing front group funded by the Koch brothers. The chairman of the group shouts: "This bastard has to be killed as a matter of political hygiene."

However, Jim Hightower, the voice of the people, tells the truth: "If five Supremes use the case, King v. Burwell, to take away health coverage for 10 million Americans they will be exposed as rank political hatchet men."

Author Ian Millhiser has already exposed them.

Sparks Tribune, May 12, 2015

Same-sex marriage triumphs

The Supreme Court ended its 2014-2015 term recently with a flurry of opinions, some good, some bad. But the most triumphant decision was the approval of gay marriage.

Justice Kennedy, writing the 5-4 majority opinion in Obergefell v. Hodges, declared "the right to marry is a fundamental right inherent to liberty." It is commanded, he said, by the due process and equal protection clauses of the 14th Amendment.

Civil rights wins and discrimination loses in the everlasting struggle for freedom in America.

Dissenting in Obergefell, Chief Justice Roberts said "those who believe in a government of laws, not of men, the majority's approach is deeply disheartening." He asked: "Just who do we think we are?"

The answer came in a letter to the New York Times from Gary Clinton of Philadelphia.

"As someone directly affected by the gay marriage ruling, I am a 64-year-old American," he wrote. "I am a seminary graduate and law school dean of students. I am a taxpayer and a voter. I am the husband of the man I fell in love with 42 years ago.

"I am a believer in America's promise and ideals. I am one of the countless gay and lesbian Americans who have waited in hope that one day our country would recognize that we deserve equality under the law. That's who I am."

Justice Scalia, 79-year-old arch-reactionary, in dissent showed how absurd he is. He called the opinion lacking "even a thin veneer in law" and said he was astounded by the "hubris reflected in the judicial putsch." Even more absurd: he denounced the opinion as a "threat to American democracy."

Scalia's "original intent" view of the Constitution is wrong-headed. The Constitution is a "living" document, constantly reflecting changing times. Same-sex marriage never occurred to the Founders but today it is a basic right.

Give Robert Barnes, columnist for the Washington Post, the last word.

"Jim Obergefell became the face of the case, when he sought to put his name on his husband's death certificate as the surviving spouse," he wrote.

"Obergefell said the ruling by the Supreme Court affirmed what millions across the country already know to be true in their hearts: that their love is equal. It is my hope that the term gay marriage will soon be a thing of the past. From this day forward it should be simply marriage.

"All Americans deserve equal dignity, respect and treatment when it comes to recognition of their relationships and families."

Court OKs Obamacare

The Supreme Court delivered a major victory to President Obama by approving his health insurance plan expanding access to individual coverage. The Affordable Care Act, passed by Congress, was the second time the court endorsed Obamacare. In the most recent case, King v. Burwell, Roberts wrote the 6-3 opinion of the court.

Obama, exulting over the decision, declared that health care is not a privilege for the few but a right for all." True. Federal appeals courts keep handing him victories, too, like the decision of the 10th circuit appeals court recently to reject a challenge by the Little Sisters of the Poor, Catholic nuns, because the act covers contraceptives.

Nevertheless, let's not rhapsodize over the victories. America, the richest country in the world, still does not have a single-payer, national health plan that progressive nations have.

EPA rule overturned

The worst ruling of the court this term overturned a regulation by the Environmental Protection Agency limiting emissions of mercury and other toxic pollutants from coal-fired power plants.

Industry groups and 20 states challenged the EPA ruling, arguing that the costs would be prohibitive. But dissenters from the 5-4 decision rightly answered that the public's health was more important than costs to industry. However, writing for the majority, antediluvian Scalia wrote: "It is not rational to impose billions of dollars in costs in return for a few dollars in health or environmental benefits."

Scalia ignored the facts presented by Mike Ludwig of Truthout: the EPA rule would annually prevent 130,000 cases of asthma attacks, 2,800 cases of chronic bronchitis, 4,700 cases of heart attacks and 130,000 visits to emergency rooms and hospital stays. Moreover, the EPA estimates that the rules would have prevented 540,000 sick days among workers annually.

Ludwig calls power plants the No. 1 source of mercury pollution, especially for people living near the nation's 600 power plants.

"Mercury contaminates waterways and the bodies of fish and other wildlife in all 50 states," he writes. "Mercury and other power-plant pollutants cause birth defects, developmental problems in children and respiratory illnesses."

After determining that reducing toxic air pollution from power plants was both "appropriate and necessary," Congress passed amendments to the Clean Air Act, which the EPA implemented in 2011.

But as so often with the Roberts Court, it rules for business, not people.

Sparks Tribune, July 21, 2015

High court surprisingly rules
for public sector unions

The death of reactionary Justice Scalia has loosened the conservative grip on the U.S. Supreme Court.

The short-handed court, divided 4-4, ruled for public sector unions in a suit by the California Teachers Association. The decision could affect the lives of millions of Americans.

"We know the wealthy extremists who pushed this case want to limit the ability of workers to have a voice, curb voting rights and restrict opportunities for women and immigrants," Mary Kay Henry, president of the Service Employees International Union, said.

The case was brought by the Center for Individual Rights, a libertarian group that pursued unusual litigation strategy, the New York Times reported.

"Responding to signals from the Supreme Court's more conservative justices, the group asked the lower courts to rule against its clients, 10 teachers and a Christian education group, so they could file an appeal in the Supreme Court as soon as possible," the Times said.

Under California law public employees who choose not to join unions must pay a "fair share" service fee.

With good reason. They get benefits such as higher wages, shorter hours and better working conditions from union negotiations.

The case, Friedrichs v. California Teachers Association, was an effort by conservative anti-union activists to cripple public-sector unions by claiming their First Amendment rights.

Justice Scalia was adamantly opposed to "fair share fees," in step with the Supreme Court commanded by Chief Justice Roberts. The pro-business Roberts court widened the gap between the rich and poor as his majority with Scalia backed the One Percenters.

A study by Richard Posner, conservative 7th circuit court of appeals chief judge, showed that the Roberts Court was the most pro-business court since World War II. Scalia was among the top 10 of business-friendly justices since that war.

Obama Refuses to Lift Cuban Embargo

As is his custom, President Obama makes nice with the leaders of foreign nations but does nothing substantive.

He visited Cuba recently, paled around with its president, Raul Castro, and pronounced a new day of openness in their relations. But, but, but.

He refused to lift the 54-year-old Cuban trade embargo. He refused to give up control of the U.S. Navy base and military prison occupying Cuban soil at Guantanamo Bay. As Castro rightly said, he cannot normalize relations with the United States until it returns Guantanamo.

"Cuba's destiny will not be decided by the United States," Castro declared. "Cuba is a sovereign nation and one with great pride."

It's more than ridiculous that huge America continues to war on tiny Cuba because it is communist.

Castro recounted the history of U.S. aggressions against Cuba, including the Bay of Pigs invasion and the nettlesome embargo that is economically costly.

As for Guantanamo, the New York Times editorialized that it was "one of the most shameful chapters in America's recent history." Closing the prison would "help restore America's standing as a champion of human rights and save U.S. taxpayers millions of dollars."

That cost: an astounding $445 million in fiscal 2015. Multiply that figure many times annually over the years and realize the full cost of keeping Gitmo open

And here is another sad statistic: out of the 800 people imprisoned in Gitmo over the past 14 years, only eight have been convicted of a crime, Aliya Hussain reported for the Center for Constitutional Rights.

Yet Republicans, eager to keep the prison open, keep howling that the prisoners are "the worst of the worst."

"An unlawful regime of indefinite and arbitrary detention continues with no end in sight," Hussain declares. "Moreover, men who have been living peacefully for years after their release still suffer hardships and the stigma of their imprisonment.

"The idea that all the men detained at Guantanamo were all sent there after being captured on 'the battlefield' by U.S. forces because 'they posed a threat' couldn't be farther from the truth.

"Most detainees were ensnared in a slipshod bounty system in which the United States paid handsome cash rewards to locals for turning over anyone who seemed 'out of place.' Many of the men who arrived in Gitmo were fleeing from--not fighting--in Afghanistan."

Hussain concludes that Gitmo has become a prison for Yemeni citizens who make up half the 91 incarcerated at last count.

Sparks Tribune, Feb. 9, 2016

Supreme Court strikes down
barbarous law

The U.S. Supreme Court ended its 2015-2016 term on a triumphant note, striking down the inhumane Texas anti-abortion law.

As Justice Ruth Bader Ginsburg wrote in a concurring opinion to the 5-3 ruling: "It is beyond belief that the Texas law could really protect the health of women."

Beyond belief, certainly, but much in keeping with oppressive, unconstitutional anti-abortion laws in many states, primarily in the Deep South.

The New York Times editorialized: "Republican lawmakers around the country are restricting or destroying constitutionally protected reproductive rights. The 2013 Texas law forced abortion clinics and their doctors to meet absurd, pointlessly strict medical standards."

Such standards were invalidated by the Supreme in 1992 by Planned Parenthood v. Casey. Obviously, the Roe v. Wade decision by the Supreme Court in 1973 that guaranteed the right to abortion has been willfully ignored.

In a polemical, retrograde dissent in the Texas case by Justice Samuel Alito, joined by Chief Justice John Robert and Justice Clarence Thomas, Alito tried vainly to justify clinic closures.

Also on the positive side, the court reaffirmed affirmative action, 4-3. The court ruled that race was just one of the many factors for admission to the University of Texas at Austin.

Justice Anthony Kennedy, writing for the majority, declared: "Considerable deference is owed to a university in defining those intangible characteristics, like student body diversity, that are central to its identity and educational mission."

But what should have been an easy, unanimous decision in the 21st century, archreactionary Thomas dissented with angry howls: "a faddish theory" and "affirmative action gone wild."

Obama Immigration Plan Stifled

The other end-of-term decisions by the court are in keeping with its many reactionary rulings over the years. The worst was a mere nine-word pronouncement in U.S. v. Texas that President Obama's immigration plan was dead.

Under the Obama plan five million undocumented immigrants would be shielded from deportation and allowed to work in the United States. Most of them are parents of American citizens.

Walter Dellinger, former acting solicitor general, rightly decried the brusque dismal of a humanitarian plea: "Seldom have the hopes of millions been crushed by so few words."

The heartless ruling left the undocumented immigrants continuing to live in fear of deportation.

Eliana Fernandez, 28, an immigrant from Ecuador, manages cases for an advocacy group. She bravely faces the illegal-immigrant dilemma: "They must step out of the shadows and speak publically as a way to humanize their plight. They must publically counter arguments that they are dangerous or a drain on America."

The court did not disclose how the justices had voted but the 4-4 vote was along the usual ideological lines with Chief Justice John Roberts joining the reactionaries.

The split vote led to laments that the court needed a ninth justice to replace Justice Scalia who died in February. True. But the sad fact is that the Republican-controlled Senate refused to hold hearings on Merrick Garland, a highly qualified appeals court judge.

The cynical Republicans felt that a Republican president elected in November would pick a conservative justice in the Scala mold.

The GOP bosses may have outsmarted themselves.

If Donald Trump is elected GOP president the nominee could be worse than the Republican chiefs bargained for. If Democrat Hillary Clinton is elected the nominee could be in the Garland vein.

Court Rules Against Graft Prosecution

In the last decision of the term, the Supreme Court ruled against graft prosecutions of public figures. Yup, although the court did not put it that bluntly. The decision was incredible enough but it overturned unanimously, 8-0, the graft conviction of Bob McConnell, former governor of Virginia.

Chief Justice Roberts labored to justify the reversal. "We cannot criminalize routine political behavior," he wrote. "Conscientious public officials arrange meetings for constituents and contact other officials on their behalf."

McDonnell, a Republican, was charged with using his office to help businessman Jonnie Williams, who had lavished luxury products, loans and vacations worth more than $175,000 on McDonnell while he was governor.

Perhaps not bribery but a decent politician would have declined such lavish gift-giving.

Another decision, 5-3, brought a fiery dissent from Justice Sonia Sotomayor. And rightly so. The ruling was purely racist.

"It is no secret that people of color are disproportionate victims of this type of scrutiny," Sotomayor wrote.

The "racist" who wrote the majority opinion? Thomas, the only black justice on the court. He was joined by fellow "racists," Chief Justice Roberts and Justices Kennedy, Alito and Stephen Breyer.

The majority ruled that evidence found by police officers after illegal stops may be used in court if the officers conducted their searches after learning defendants had outstanding arrest warrants.

Thomas said such searches do not violate the Fourth

Amendment when the warrant is valid and unconnected to the conduct that prompted the search.

Sotomayor said that "the court had vastly expanded police power." Indeed it had.

Sparks Tribune, July 26, 2016

History

Kissinger's air power diplomacy

The United States still practices the evil spawned by Henry Kissinger: endless wars and imperialistic diplomacy by air power.

Greg Grandin, author of "Kissinger's Shadow," tells the theme of his book in a news analysis for TomDispatch. Kissinger was national security adviser and secretary of state under President Richard Nixon.

"Within days of Nixon's inauguration in 1969, Kissinger asked the Pentagon to lay out his bombing options in Indochina," Grandin writes. "The previous president, Lyndon Johnson, suspended the bombing campaign against North Vietnam in hope of negotiating a broader cease fire."

But Nixon and Kissinger were eager to re-launch the campaign. They ordered bombing across the border in Cambodia after cooking up a rational that they sought to destroy North Vietnam supplies, depots and bases.

They wrongly believed such an onslaught might force Hanoi, capital of North Vietnam, to make concessions at the negotiating table. It was the beginning of monstrous "killing fields" genocide in Cambodia.

Nixon had been elected to end the Vietnam War but, fearful of an adverse reaction from Congress for bombing a neutral nation, Nixon labeled the plan top secret and resorted to deception. He had the B-52 runs over South Vietnam switched to Cambodian targets.

Kissinger directed the sites to be bombed while thoroughly enjoying the role of bombardier. He beamed at reports of huge bomb craters. Dr. K approved 3,875 Cambodia bombing raids in 1969 and 1970.

The U.S. military dropped 6 billion tons of bombs on Southeast Asia by order of "bombardier" Kissinger. His order to blast "anything that flies or everything that moves" was carried out. The Finnish Government Committee of Inquiry put the Cambodian deaths at 600,000.

John Pilger, reporting for Truthout, said "the bombing of Cambodia unleashed a torrent of suffering from which the country has never recovered."

Dr. K's most recent apologia for his crimes was a book he wrote ironically entitled "World Order." Tell that to the people of Cambodia, Vietnam, Laos, Chile and East Timor victimized by his "statecraft."

They were crimes undertaken at a great distance by an imperial power. The nations victimized were helpless to strike back. This horrible truth was usually missing from most journalistic reports, assuring the unawareness of most Americans.

Making Abortions Easier

Laws in California and Oregon will soon allow pharmacists to prescribe pills, patches and rings for birth control without having a doctor's prescription. Patients in those states need only be screened for risk factors such as smoking and blood clots.

The pills and devices are safe. Therefore, 48 other states should pass similar legislation. As the New York Times editorialized recently, "these laws would help many women get the contraceptives they need."

Oregon's new law takes effect in January, California's in April. A pharmacy chain is seeking a similar law in Nevada. A drive is underway for such legislation in New Mexico.

Don't Dontate to Fat Cats

The very names prompt tender feelings about Christmas donations: United Nations Children's Fund, The American Red Cross, the March of Dimes and Goodwill. But think again before you donate to them at yuletide or any other time.

Marsha Evans, Red Cross CEO, makes $650,000 in yearly salary plus expenses. The March of Dimes gives away just 10 cents of every charitable dollar received. Caryl Stern, the CEO of UNICEF, reaps $1,200,000 a year plus expenses and a Rolls Royce. Less than five cents a dollar goes to charity.

Goodwill owner and CEO, Mark Curran, nabs $2.3 million a year for good clothes given free to Goodwill. United Way President gets a "measly" $375,000 a year along with numerous expense benefits.

These staggering figures come from a highly reliable source: James Spangler, public watchdog extraordinaire who monitors charities. Spangler recommends giving to Salvation Army and Doctors Without Borders as the best charitable organizations because most of the donations to them actually reach the needy.

Down with Monarchy

Jeremy Corbyn, staunch republican who is the leftist leader of the British Labor Party, refused to sing "God Save the Queen" at a recent Buckingham Palace ceremony. He also refused to speak to Queen Elizabeth II on bended knee.

Traditionalists were shocked. Apparently they never heard of the French Revolution.

The monarchy is not just centuries obsolete, it costs millions to the few nations that still have them. They are used merely for pomp and circumstance to please the hoi polloi. Sensible nations long since have shed such antiquities.

Principle Before Glory

Patricia Canning Todd, who died recently, was one of the long forgotten pioneers of the women's liberation movement.

She won four tennis Grand Slam singles titles in 1947

and 1948 but gave up a chance to win a fifth in 1948 when she refused to play in the French Open final because the match was relegated to a side court.

"Todd played relentlessly, using a devilish backhand to beat such stars as Gussie Moran and Louise Brough," a New York Times obit reported. She was 93.

Public Intellectual Non-Existent

For nearly two decades "public intellectual" (PI) has become a terrible cliché.

Here's the latest usage by author Pankaj Mishra in a Bookends column for the Sunday New York Times: "The most influential public intellectual today is Pope Francis." Francis is not an intellectual. He is extremely popular worldwide but not a so-called PI.

Noam Chomsky, professor at Massachusetts Institute of Technology and prolific author of books and articles, is highly intellectual but not a PI. Few people are.

Sparks Tribune, Dec. 8, 2015

Hearst defied newspaper truth

SAN SIMEON, Calif.--The nearby Hearst Castle, halfway between San Francisco and Los Angeles, is a spectacle worth visiting. It is perched on 240,000 acres of a high hill overlooking the Pacific.

But as a journalism historian and journalism history teacher for five decades, I detest William Randolph Hearst. He was first with the worst. He defied a newspaper's first principle: the truth in the news.

But the truth was of no concern to him. Circulation and listenership were all that mattered. His American empire, the largest in the world, included 28 newspapers, the five major magazines and 73 radio stations. His "yellow journalism" invented sensational stories, faked interviews and ran doctored pictures.

Myth has it that Hearst started the Spanish-American War in 1898. His illustrator, Frederic Remington, supposedly telegraphed him saying everything is quiet in Cuba so he wanted to come home. Hearst reportedly replied: "Please remain. You furnish the pictures and I'll furnish the war."

Never happened. But the fable illustrates how Hearst distorted the news.

Julia Morgan, great architect who designed the castle, was hampered by Hearst's constant changes, which undermined her genius.

Hearst did the same thing with his newspapers. If in Chicago, for instance, he would order four changes in the bulldog edition before it went to press. (Bulldog is newspaper terminology for the first edition).

His mistress, Marion Davies, rightly lambasted him in the film "Citizen Kane," taken from a biographer's book title, "Citizen Hearst." Davies told him with a winning stutter: "All you do is talk about your g-g-god-damn circulation."

Hearst boosted her career almost daily in his papers although she could not sing on key. The Italian singing maestro in "Citizen Kane" shouts out in exasperation at Ms. Davies during one lesson: "No! No! No! No! No!"

"Citizen Kane," starring Orson Welles, is one of the great American films. The opening is foreboding, portentous and dramatic. Welles' deep voice quotes the opening lines of the Coleridge poem "Kubla Khan": "In Xanadu did Kubla Khan / A stately treasure dome decree." The Hearst Castle, a "treasure dome," looms high overhead in a darkened sky.

The film is marred by frequent reference to the phony "rosebud" theme. Rosebud was the name Hearst gave his sled in childhood.

Hearst, angered by Welles' unflattering portrait, used his enormous influence to halt RKO's release of the movie. Fortunately, he failed. The movie shows how Hearst had the castle built, not out of passion as his propagandists claim, but as a monument to himself.

As for visiting the Hearst Castle today, there is not a single room in the palace that is comfortable. Too grandiose, too lacking in taste as with so much of the art Hearst bought in Europe.

A 500-year-old tapestry, "The Deer Hunt," is an exception. It enlivens the sitting room with a vibrant green in contrast to the browned-out, dull tapestries hanging nearby.

In the entrance visitors are shown a 30-minute propaganda film about how magnificent the palace is. In the castle store none of the many critical books on Hearst are available. Nor is "Citizen Kane."

The beach at San Simeon compensates. The ocean breakers constantly roll in, crashing on the beach. Pelicans fly overhead. Sandpipers and willets scurry after prey along the beach.

Driving north, we stopped at Seal Rock. About 10

seals were basking in the sun. A pair was making love in the nearby water, tenderly pushing each other's nose.

Continuing north to Monterey, we stopped to watch an elk herd. A bull elk with a huge rack was herding the females while their kids stood by patiently. We drove along Route 1, a twisting, hazardous, narrow road requiring the skilled driver we had.

Monterey. Steinbeck country. John Steinbeck, author, "The Grapes of Wrath" and "Of Mice and Men." Excellent novels made into good films. Finally, I-80 and home.

Home! What a joy to be home after journey's end.

Worker Bill of Rights

Voters in Spokane, Wash., will decide Nov. 3 on a Worker Bill of Rights.

It proposes the "right to a family wage when employed by a large employer" and equal pay for equal work. It also guarantees the right not to be wrongly fired.

The family wage proviso is the first anywhere in America although cities like San Francisco, Los Angeles and Seattle have a $15 minimum wage.

A family wage is the amount needed to meet the basic needs of a two-person household. That is, a single parent and one child require $45,797 annually, according to the Economic Policy Institute.

While the bill of rights would affect only one percent of Spokane establishments, such a law would impact the Seattle hospitals, casino, energy firms and Walmart.

A report by Mario Vasquez of Truthout points out the huge inequality "of a woman who has worked full time, year around in the past 12 months, making an average of $9,124 less than Spokane men with similar on-the-job experience."

All working women know it is still a men's world.

Sparks Tribune, Oct. 6, 2015

Book, existentialism baloney

There is nothing so absurd but some philosopher has said it.

Cicero

The absurdity of philosophy has ancient roots for good reason: it is true. If you want proof read the history of existentialism by Sarah Bakewell.

Her new book, "At the Existential Café," even carries an absurd subtitle: "Freedom, Being and Apricot Cocktails."

"Jean-Paul Sartre mixed his ideas with those of the earlier Danish philosopher Soren Kierkegaard to apply phenomenology to people's lives. However, he did it in a more exciting, personal way. Sartre thus became the founding father of a philosophy that became international in impact: modern existentialism."

Understand that?

The book gets worse a few pages later:

"The dizziness of freedom and the anguish of experience were embarrassments. Biography was out because life itself was out. Experience was out. Philosophy was turned back into an abstract landscape, stripped of the active, impassioned beings who occupied it in the existential era."

Capiche?

Author Bakewell admits existentialism is hard to define then uses nine meanings to define it. One of them is insane-asylum gibberish: "I am only free within situations, which can include factors in my own biology and psychology as well as physical, historical and social variables of the world into which I have been thrown."

More gobbledygook chosen at random from the book:

• Sartre on existentialism: "It is perfectly true, as philosophers say, that life must be understood backwards. But they forget the other proposition: that it must be lived forward. It becomes evident that life can never be really understood in time. The reason is that at no particular moment can I find the necessary resting place from which to understand it."

• Sartre on existentialism in three words: "Existence precedes essence."

• Bakewell: "In this chapter we meet revolutionaries, outsiders and seekers after authenticity." (Does it take complicated philosophizing to be authentic?)

• Sartre: "The eyes of the least-favored idea is as radical as other-directed ethics and more radical than communism." (Huh?)

• More "deep thought" by Blakewell: "The bloom of experience and communication lies at the heart of the human misery. It is what makes possible the living, conscious embodied beings that we are. It also is the subject to which phenomenologists and existentialists devoted much of their research." (Research of garbage?)

"The existentialists at the café peered at a sugar cube from all angles. To each of them the sugar presented itself differently." (Oh, my, my.)

• Kierkegaard defined existential as "denoting thought concerning the problems of human existence." (At last! Something understandable.)

Among the many other cast of characters and their descriptions in the book:

• Dostoevsky, Russian novelist and proto-existentialist.

• Hegel, German philosopher whose "Phenomenology of Spirit" and dialectical theory influenced most of the existentialists.

• Giacometti, Italian-Swiss sculptor, friend of Sartre and Simone de Beauvoir. He sketched Sartre.

• Nietzsche, German philosopher, philologist and proto-existentialist.

• Juliette Greco, French singer, actor and existentialist muse.

Albert Camus is the most understandable of

existentialists and practically the only one worth reading.

In Camus' "The Stranger" his protagonist is about to be executed. A shriving priest visits his cell but is angrily told by the stranger: "None of your certainties is worth one strand of a woman's hair." The truth is clear and ringing.

A terrible flaw in the book is the biographer's besetting sin: "possibly," "may have," "must have thought," "it would seem" and "apparently."

Bakewell does tell this truth: "We still find a nostalgic romance in the old images of Sartre at his café table, the turbaned Beauvoir and the brooding Camus with his collar turned up."

Aside from all the nonsense, Bakewell's pages are strewn with pictures of street scenes, people and famous philosophers without captions. None is identified although we know--or can guess--the names of some.

The acknowledgements page is copious with praise and thanks for all the "insightful" editing of friends and advisers yet all committed the elementary crime of any book or newspaper publisher: failing to identify photos.

Here is my final word on existentialism. Sartre wrote in his play "No Exit": "Hell is other people." That is understandable and people can relate to it.

Sparks Tribune, April 5, 2016

Pullman car workers honored

All presidents nowadays burnish their credentials with history buffs and conservationists by creating national monuments.

President Obama is no exception. The Antiquities Act of 1906 allows presidents to protect historic or ecologically significant sites without congressional approval.

Obama recently named three new national monuments, bringing his total to 16. They are: a site on Chicago's South Side dedicated to the labor movement, a prison camp in Hawaii that held World War II prisoners and a whitewater rafting area in Colorado.

Pullman National Monument

Pullman honors the neighborhood built by industrialist George Pullman in the late 19th century for workers to manufacture luxurious sleeping cars. It also hired former slaves to work as porters, waiters and maids on the cars.

But when a severe recession hit, Pullman slashed wages. Workers began to suffer so they joined the American Railway Union organized by Eugene Debs. The union called a strike in 1894, which affected 250,000 workers on 29 railroads in 27 states.

The workers rightly complained that their pay was cut but the rents they paid in the Pullman company town stayed the same. Debs wanted a general strike of union members. But Samuel Gompers, reactionary head of the American Federation of Labor, said no.

Pullman hired strikebreakers to take the place of the Debs team. The biggest strikebreaker of all strikebreakers joined the fray on the side of Pullman: President Grover Cleveland. He got an injunction in federal court against the strikers and brought in 14,000 U.S. troops.

Two heroes emerged: Debs and Philip Randolph. Debs, ignoring the court order, was convicted and sent to prison. Clarence Darrow, the great criminal defense lawyer, defended Debs at his unjust trial.

Fifty years later Randolph formed the Brotherhood of Sleeping Car Porters, the first African American union. Later Randolph became active in the burgeoning civil rights movement.

Honolulu National Monument

Located on Oahu Island, this monument housed Japanese-American citizens, one of the most shameful episodes of American history. Civil liberties of loyal Americans were suspended after the Japanese attack on Pearl Harbor. (Loyal Japanese-American citizens were also shamefully interned in California during the war.)

Browns Canyon National Monument

Outdoors and wildlife groups were delighted by creation of this monument, declaring it offers a whitewater rafting, hunting and fishing paradise. Browns Canyon is on a 21,500-acre wilderness stretch of the Arkansas River with rugged granite cliffs, colorful rock outcroppings and dramatic mountain views.

The area already attracts 100,000 tourists annually with many more to come now that it is a monument.

Shills for movies, books

I rarely go to movie theaters, preferring to watch great films of the past on DVDs and videos. But I went to a downtown Reno flick house recently to see "Wild" because it got rave reviews in the New York Times. I also went because I love the outdoors and its wildlife.

The film, based on a memoir by Cheryl Strayed, has spectacular scenery but is otherwise a flop. I can't remember being so disappointed in a movie, walking out after an hour of tedium.

It stars Reese Witherspoon supposedly hiking the 1,100-mile Pacific Coast National Scenic Trail from the Mojave Desert in California to the forests of Oregon.

We see little of her hiking except for a few trail scenes showing a rattlesnake, a fox and ancient Joshua trees. Another true scene that any Nevada hiker can appreciate: she crushes and smells sagebrush for its sweet scent.

But, oh my, the constant annoying flashbacks about Cheryl Strayed's troubled childhood, her self-destructive behavior, her addiction to heroin, her sex life, the break up of her marriage, her pregnancy by an unknown father and the death of her mother from cancer. Reminiscences ad nauseam.

Cheryl is such a neophyte that she buys lots of hiking and camping gear but doesn't know how to use them. Nevertheless, the film spends the first 10 minutes boring the viewer. It shows her stowing the bulky gear and her difficulty heisting the enormous pack on the back of her tiny frame.

Moreover, Cheryl seldom hikes. She's hitchhiking, sticking out her thumb and accepting long rides from seedy characters or getting a long lecture and care package from a well-meaning passer by.

The film epitomizes what I have long felt about movie and book reviewers: they don't tell the searing truth. They are shills for movies and books.

Sparks Tribune, March 24, 2015

The Media

Reporter creates bogus war

Lincoln purportedly said to Harriet Beecher Stowe: "So you're the little woman who wrote the book that made this great war." The Lincoln story about Stowe's "Uncle Tom's Cabin" is apocryphal. But there is no doubt that the Civil War was absolutely necessary.

Conversely, Judith Miller, New York Times reporter, was the little woman who made the Iraq II War. That war was absolutely unnecessary.

Miller's tale was exactly what President G.W. Bush wanted: war. All Bush needed was the powerful credential of the influential Times. He got it. The editors and Judy Miller got everlasting shame.

Her series of stories talked darkly of chemical and biological weapons and possible nuclear materials in Iraq. A mushroom cloud loomed. Iraq leader Saddam Hussein was an evil man. He posed a threat and must be eliminated. Fantasies all. But the Times war drum gave Bush the cover he needed.

Miller has just come out with a book, "The Story: a Reporter's Journey," defending the indefensible.

She became a Times staffer in 1977 largely because the Times was male-dominated and faced a sex discrimination suit. She was a raw reporter with little experience. An editor bluntly told her she was sloppy.

Nevertheless, Times editors made her an investigative reporter, a position far over her head. In a review of her book, Terry McDermott, former Los Angeles Times national correspondent, wrote:

"She had built her career on access. She describes finding and cultivating powerful sources. The agenda that comes through most strongly is a desire to land on the front page."

She often did.

Andy Barbano, Sparks Tribune columnist, recalls the

"most egregious sin" of her "investigative" reporting: "Getting a leak from Vice President Dick Cheney's office that Iraq had a weapon of mass destruction (WMD) than 'confirming' it by calling the same office."

Another Millerism: during the war Miller was the only reporter embedded with the military team charged with finding Iraq's WMD. She was figuratively in bed with the military.

Miller and the Times live in infamy. America lives with the infamy of a gratuitous war in Iraq.

More infamy: America's disastrous wars in Iraq, Afghanistan and Pakistan have killed more than 1.3 million people and caused enormous internal turmoil.

A San Francisco doctor, Robert Gould, writes about a report called the "Body Count" recently published by Physicians for Social Responsibility: "It has been politically important to downplay U.S. responsibility for the massive carnage and destruction in the region. But America needs to admit responsibility for the enormous cost of the wars in lives and money."

U.S. meddling in the region is still going on. No wonder America is despised in the Middle East.

WANTED: MORE BOWE BERGDAHLS

Which brings us to Sgt. Bowe Bergdahl. The Taliban held him for five years after he disappeared from his Army post in Afghanistan in 2009. Released to the United States, he has been charged by Pentagon brass with "misbehavior before the enemy." He faces a court martial and life in prison.

Amy Goodman, public broadcast commentator, reflects bitterly: "Meanwhile, the architects of the disastrous wars in Iraq and Afghanistan remain untried."

Robert Musil, who has written sympathetically about Vietnam War deserters, writes: "Where is all that rhetoric about 'we support our troops'? Bergdahl has suffered a lot. Where are understanding, compassion and humanity? I think that is the proper response to an American kid stranded in the middle of Afghanistan who feels he had no choice but to leave his unit."

Another bitter critic says: "The main reason the military is going after him is they don't want to cough up hundreds of thousands of dollars in back pay. This is ironic because the government since 2001 has wasted trillions in Afghanistan and given millions to its warlords.

"The evidence that he's responsible for the death of six U.S. soldiers is tenuous. The blame for these deaths should be placed on the military for sending soldiers into a war that never should have occurred."

Rory Fanning, a former Army Ranger in Afghanistan, wrote a book last year called "Worth Fighting For." In it he writes: "We need a million more Bowe Bergdhals. Anybody with common sense and moral fortitude would say: 'This is ridiculous. I'm not going to fight this war.' "

Fanning concludes: "It's fear-mongering propping up perpetual wars. Recruitment is down. People are beginning to realize we're not fighting for freedom or democracy but for empire."

The anti-war expressions are all too true. But another truth doesn't bode well for Bergdahl. Georges Clemenceau, prime minster of France during World War I, said it best: "Military justice is to justice what military music is to music."

Sparks Tribune, May 5, 2015

CPSIA information can be obtained
at www.ICGtesting.com
Printed in the USA
FSOW01n0522120816
23518FS